9.95

D0842688

CROSS-CULTURAL
ENCOUNTERS
AND CONFLICTS

STUDIES IN MIDDLE EASTERN HISTORY
Bernard Lewis, Itamar Rabinovich,
and Roger Savory
General Editors

The Turban for the Crown
The Islamic Revolution in Iran
Said Amir Arjomand

The Arab Press in the Middle East
A History
Ami Ayalon

Iran's First Revolution
*Shi'ism and the Constitutional
Revolution of 1905–1909*
Mangol Bayat

Saddam's Word
Political Discourse in Iraq
Ofra Bengio

Islamic Reform
*Politics and Social Change in
Late Ottoman Syria*
David Dean Commins

King Hussein and the Challenge
of Arab Radicalism
Jordan, 1955–1967
Uriel Dann

Nasser's "Blessed Movement"
*Egypt's Free Officers and the
July Revolution*
Joel Gordon

The Young Turks in Opposition
M. Şükrü Hanioğlu

Cross-Cultural Encounters and
Conflicts
Charles Issawi

The Fertile Crescent, 1800–1914
A Documentary Economic History
Edited by Charles Issawi

The Making of Saudi Arabia,
1916–1936
*From Chieftaincy to
Monarchical State*
Joseph Kostiner

Eunuchs and Sacred Boundaries in
Islamic Society
Shaun Marmon

The Imperial Harem
*Women and Sovereignty in the
Ottoman Empire*
Leslie Peirce

From Abdullah to Hussein
Jordan in Transition
Robert B. Satloff

Other volumes are in preparation.

CROSS-CULTURAL

ENCOUNTERS

AND CONFLICTS

Charles Issawi

New York   Oxford

Oxford University Press

1998

Oxford University Press

Oxford   New York
Athens   Auckland   Bangkok   Bogota   Bombay   Buenos Aires
Calcutta   Cape Town   Dar es Salaam   Delhi   Florence   Hong Kong
Istanbul   Karachi   Kuala Lumpur   Madras   Madrid   Melbourne
Mexico City   Nairobi   Paris   Singapore   Taipei   Tokyo   Toronto   Warsaw

and associated companies in
Berlin   Ibadan

Published by Oxford University Press, Inc.
198 Madison Avenue, New York, New York 10016

Oxford is a registered trademark of Oxford University Press

Library of Congress Cataloging-in-Publication Data
Issawi, Charles Philip.
Cross-cultural encounters and conflicts / Charles Issawi.
p.   cm.—(Studies in Middle Eastern history)
ISBN 0-19-511813-8
1. Middle East—Civilization.   2. Acculturation—Middle East.
3. Culture conflict—Middle East.   4. East and West.   5. Europe—
Civilization.   I. Title.   II. Series: Studies in Middle Eastern
history (New York, N.Y.)
DS57.I85 1998
956—dc21   97-34739

1 3 5 7 9 8 6 4 2

Printed in the United States of America
on acid-free paper

For Janina

ACKNOWLEDGMENTS

Most of these essays have appeared in various journals and symposia and are reproduced by kind permission of the respective editors and publishers.

Chapter 2—*Journal of Interdisciplinary History* (20:2, Encounter Ltd., London, autumn 1989), published by Massachusetts Institute of Technology.

Chapter 3—*Encounter* (72, No. 3, May 1989) published by Encounter Ltd., London.

Chapter 4—*Princeton Papers in Near Eastern Studies* (No. 3, 1994), published by the Department of Near Eastern Studies, Princeton University.

Chapter 5—L. Carl Brown (ed.), *Imperial Legacy* (Columbia University Press, New York, 1996).

Chapter 6—Dimitri Gondicas and Charles Issawi (eds.), *Ottoman Greeks in the Age of Nationalism* (Darwin Press, Princeton, 1997).

Chapter 7—*The American Scholar* (Summer 1989, Autumn 1989), published by the United Chapters of Phi Beta Kappa.

Chapter 8—*The American Scholar* (Summer 1981), published by the United Chapters of Phi Beta Kappa.

Lastly, a more personal acknowledgement. I should like to express my heartfelt thanks to Bernard Lewis for his help in the preparation and publication of this book. Being his colleague and friend has been a great privilege.

CONTENTS

CROSS-CULTURAL
ENCOUNTERS
AND CONFLICTS

Gottes ist der Orient!
Gottes ist der Okzident!
Nord-und südliches Gelände
Ruht in Frieden seiner Hände.
Goethe

To God belongs the East
To God belongs the West,
North and southern lands
Rest in the peace of His hands.

INTRODUCTION

This book is mainly concerned with the way some of the world's major cultures have perceived, and interacted with, each other in the course of the last two thousand years.

In one form or another, this subject has fascinated me since my early years. I grew up in a Westernized, Christian, Syrian family, in the cosmopolitan, but essentially Egyptian, city of Cairo. From early childhood I was deeply conscious of the differences between "*Frank-ish*" (European) mores and ways of thinking and behaving and local ones. Ours was also a multilingual family in which Arabic, French, and English were spoken.[1] I was educated in foreign schools (mainly British, but also French) in Cairo and Alexandria and went from there to Oxford. Later, I served in the United Nations Secretariat in New York. This gave me further occasions to reflect upon contrasts between the two cultures, and also those between British and French ways. The essays in the book reflect my thinking on this subject in the last 15 or 20 years.

Chapter 1 ("The Clash of Cultures in the Near East") examines conflicts in the region between the Greek and Semitic cultures 2,000 years ago and between the Western and Muslim cultures during the last 200 years. In both cases an alien, dynamic, and intellectually more advanced society dominated a less advanced, evoking two kinds of responses—the Herodian and the Zealot, to use Arnold Toynbee's convenient terms.

On the one hand, a small, but very influential, group drawn

mainly from the upper strata—eager to modernize its society in order to assure its survival—was fascinated by the foreign culture and adopted its values, its ways of behavior, and often its speech. On the other hand, the mass of society showed indifference, or dislike. And within the latter, a small but very active group displayed intense zeal in denouncing and combating foreign influences and customs. The chapter discusses the synthesis that was achieved in the past and speculates on whether something similar will ensue today.

Chapter 2 ("Empire Builders, Culture Makers, and Cultural Imprinters") starts by surveying the distribution of the main language groups—Chinese, Indian, Russian, Anglo-Saxon, Latin European, Latin American, and Arab—that between them account for some two-thirds of the world's population. These language divisions largely coincide with those of what might be called "popular" culture (i.e., food, dress, architecture, and religion). The chapter surveys the steps by which these cultures attained their present locations and dimensions. Analysis of the process shows that the brilliance of a people's "high" culture is not a major factor in the imprinting of its language and popular culture on other peoples. Capacity for empire building, that is, the creation of durable and widespread political structures, is more significant since it provides the framework within which the popular culture can be imprinted on indigenous populations and immigrants—North and South America and Russia provide good examples. But the most important factor seems to be the presence of a proselytizing religion, such as Christianity or Islam, which can "imprint" itself and its accompanying mores and institutions.

Chapters 3 and 4 ("Shelley and the Near East" and "Ibn Khaldun on Ancient History: A Study in Sources") discuss the way two remarkable, but very dissimilar, men—Shelley and the Arab historian and sociologist Ibn Khaldun—looked at a foreign culture. In addition to being a marvelous lyric poet, Shelley was an accomplished linguist and very well read in philosophy, history, and politics. His interest in the Near East arose chiefly from his passionate Philhellenism, which made him an ardent champion of Greek independence and opponent of Ottoman rule, but his interest extended beyond that and his observations on India, Persia, Egypt, Syria, Arabia, and proto-Zionism are acute.

Ibn Khaldun's profound historical and sociological observations were based on his reading of Arab-Muslim history but, relatively late in life, he came across an Arabic translation of Orosius, *Historiarum Adversus Paganos,* a fifth century work, which greatly enlarged his view of Roman and, more generally, ancient history. The differences between his earlier *Muqaddimah* and later *'Ibar* are striking and are discussed at length, as is the nature of his sources. His knowledge of the ancient world is contrasted with that of representative medieval West European and Byzantine historians.

The two following chapters concern the Ottoman Empire. Chapter 5 ("The Ottoman Economic Legacy") discusses the Ottomans' failure to develop an economic theory of their own, or to assimilate the one that was emerging in Europe. I also discuss the inadequacy of some Ottoman economic institutions, which may be partly explained by the structure of Ottoman society and the political power enjoyed by the bureaucracy and army as opposed to the producing classes, and more particularly the farmers and craftsmen. Until the very end of the empire, Ottoman policy was primarily concerned with fiscal considerations and with the interest of consumers, or more precisely, the court, bureaucracy, and army, and little or no attempt was made to stimulate production or exports by such Mercantilist measures as were being taken in contemporary Europe. These attitudes and practices were passed on to the Arab successor states. One very important exception may, however, be noted. Ottoman laws regarding minerals gave the right to the subsoil to the state and not to the owner of the soil, as in Anglo-Saxon law. This proved ideally suited to petroleum development in this century and, together with favorable natural conditions, explains the phenomenal productivity and profitability of the Gulf petroleum industry.

Chapter 6 ("The Greeks in the Middle East") examines an important aspect of the *millet* system that has characterized the region since the rise of Islam and even earlier. I study the great economic power enjoyed by the millets (notably Greeks, Armenians, and Jews) at length as well as the part they played in the social and cultural fields and examine the swift decline of these millets at the end of the nineteenth and beginning of the twentieth century.

In the next two chapters the focus shifts to Western Europe, and specifically to some aspects of the secular rivalry between its two leading countries, France and Britain. Chapter 7 ("The Costs of the French Revolution") discusses the demographic, economic, and other losses caused by the French Revolution and the ensuing wars. In the eighteenth century, France had been growing at least as fast as Britain, but the disruption caused by the revolution and wars set it back and gave Britain a lead that lasted well into this century and is only now being overcome.

Chapter 8 ("The Struggle for Linguistic Hegemony") traces the gradual replacement of French by English as a world language. In the seventeenth century, the ascendancy of French was ensured by the overwhelming military and political predominance of France, by its enormous wealth and rich culture, and by the fascination with Louis XIV and his court, which formed a model for European monarchs. But new forces slowly shifted the balance. Britain became the leading commercial, financial, and industrial nation. The extension of the British Empire was accompanied by that of the English language. The expansion of the United States meant an enormous accretion of numbers and power for English speakers. The rise of British (followed by that of American) science and technology was another favorable factor. Lastly, American participation in the two world wars and the emergence of the United States as the leading superpower finally tipped the balance.

Chapter 9 ("Change in Western Perceptions of the Orient Since the Eighteenth Century") examines a very interesting phenomenon: the profound change in the West's perception of the Orient between the eighteenth and nineteenth centuries, from an attitude of respect and even admiration to one of contempt. The term "Orient" here refers to India, China, and Islam, the first two being treated more lightly and the last more extensively. I analyze the various factors that produced the change: the revival of Christianity in Britain and France, which made them less tolerant of other religions; the military, political, and economic domination they achieved over Asia and Africa; the overwhelming technological superiority of the West and the increase in respect for women, which made such practices as footbinding or polygamy—not to mention suttee—seem intolerable and almost sufficient, by themselves, to condemn these cultures. I bring the analysis up to date by discussing developments in the nineteenth and twentieth centuries.

Note

1. I have discussed this matter more fully in "Growing up Different," to be published in a book on Middle Eastern childhood edited by Elizabeth Fernea.

ONE

THE CLASH OF CULTURES
IN THE NEAR EAST

The Near East is, unfortunately, very much in the news nowa-
days, with murders, kidnappings, car bombings, wars, and—
the subject of this chapter—outbursts of Islamic fundamentalism or,
as I prefer to call it, Islamic revivalism or radicalism. These convulsions are the result of, among other factors, the clash of cultures in
the region. It may help to understand this phenomenon by looking
at a similar one that took place in the Near East some 2,000 years
ago.

For 1,000 years, from Alexander to the Arab conquest, the Near
East was subjected to the very powerful influence of one of the world's
most brilliant civilizations, the Greek. This continued after the Romans took over, since they did not attempt to replace Greek with
Latin as the official language. Alexander had had a noble dream, the
Hellenization of the East and the symbiosis of its peoples with the
Greeks. In addition to encouraging intermarriage between his Macedonian soldiers and generals and Asian women, and setting the example, he founded over 20 cities—from Alexandria in Egypt to several
Alexandrias in Afghanistan and beyond the Oxus. His Seleucid successors founded another 70 colonies or so. In its new environment,
particularly in Alexandria and Pergamum, Hellenistic civilization
reached amazing heights in mathematics, science, medicine, literature, the plastic arts, and various branches of scholarship. Later,
Beirut was to have the leading law school of the Roman Empire.

But the cultural impact on the indigenous populations was in no way commensurate with this achievement. In Egypt one of the world's most rigorously planned economies was set up, the country's resources were exploited with remarkable efficiency, and various measures were taken to expand production and trade. But no serious attempt seems to have been made to Hellenize the Egyptians. Only one town other than Alexandria was founded, race relations seem to have been bad, and eventually the Egyptians reacted to their exploitation by strikes and revolts. Under Roman rule conditions were, if anything, worse. In Mesopotamia the Greeks colonized on a larger scale, and in its way Seleucia-on-the-Tigris could rival Alexandria. The Greeks also showed great interest in, and borrowed from, Babylonian mathematics and astronomy. But, to quote from Michael Grant:

> However, these instances of cultural movement between the Greeks and the land of the Tigris and Euphrates are not only somewhat specialized but form an almost wholly one-way traffic. Despite all the impetus towards collaboration exerted by Seleucia on the Tigris and other colonies, the people of Mesopotamia and the territories around it remained little affected by Hellenization, because the roots of their own civilizations were so deep and irremovable: and there were too few Greeks in the country to make a serious impact.[1]

As for Asia Minor: "Perhaps the city of Pergamum spread rather more Hellenization round its fringes than Alexandria ever succeeded in doing. Yet in the last resort, like Alexandria, it was merely the Greek facade of a state consisting of non-Greek natives, who practised their own religious cults in villages that were still the principal economic and social units of the kingdom."[2] Iran was even less affected:

> As for the Persians, even if a noble might occasionally leave his fortified country mansion and muster up a superficial Greek social habit or two, they were, taken in all, not Hellenized in the slightest degree. Hellenization failed to compete in Iran. Generations of peace and stability might conceivably have made the story different. But these peaceful epochs never materialized.[3]

Syria presents a much more interesting and complex phenomenon. Greek colonization was much more intense than elsewhere, and many more cities were founded, particularly in the northern half of the country. Moreover, in order to gain collaborators in the task of holding together their far-flung empire, the Seleucids gave the indigenous peoples certain rights and even granted Greek civic charters to whole native communities. Let me again quote Grant: "Syria's record of comparatively successful Hellenization is illustrated by a remarkable series of Greek philosophers it produced, especially Stoics. Yet the land remained essentially bicultural."[4]

It is in Syria, and more particularly among its Jewish population, whose history is better documented, that we see the twofold reactions to Hellenization that Arnold Toynbee characterized as the Zealot and Herodian:

> The 'Zealot' is the man who takes refuge from the unknown in the familiar and when he joins battle with a stranger who practises superior tactics and employs formidable new-fangled weapons, and finds himself getting the worst of the encounter, he responds by practising his own traditional art of war with abnormally scrupulous exactitude. . . . The 'Herodian' is the man who acts on the principle that the most effective way to guard against danger of the unknown is to master its secret; and, when he finds himself in the predicament of being confronted by a more highly skilled and better armed opponent, he responds by discarding his traditional art of war and learning to fight his enemy with the enemy's own tactics and own weapons. If 'Zealotism' is a form of archaism evoked by foreign pressure, 'Herodianism' is a form of cosmopolitanism evoked by that self-same external agency."[5]

Among the Jews there were many who outheroded Herod in their admiration for Greek or Roman culture; this comes out clearly in the *Book of the Maccabees*. Some Jews made notable contributions to it, such as Philo the philosopher, who, apparently, could not read Hebrew,[6] and Josephus the historian. Others, like the high priest Jason and his successor, Menelaus, paid it the compliment of adopting Greek names and proposing to establish a gymnasium and other heathenish institutions in Jerusalem itself. They had their counterparts among the other Syrians, for example, the philosopher Zeno, who was a Phoenician from Cyprus, the philosopher Posidonius of Apamea, Cicero's teacher, and the poet Meleager, the satirist Menippus, and the philosopher Philodemus, all three from Gadara in Transjordan, a city that deserves to be remembered for other things than the Gadarene swine. Meleager sent the following message from his imaginary tomb: "If you are a Syrian, *Salam*; if you are a Phoenician, *Naidios* [the word is certainly corrupt]; if you are a Greek, *Chaire*; and say the same yourself."[7] And later there was the witty writer Lucian, who learned Greek as a second language.[8] And there must have been many thousands, or tens of thousands, whose Greek names contrast with the Semitic ones of their fathers and who spoke and wrote Greek and frequented gynmasia. Under the Romans the two leading jurists, Ulpian and Papinian, were probably Syrians.

The outstanding Zealots were first the Maccabees, whose guerilla wars finally won them independence from the Greeks. Their successors soon turned Herodian and went in for much Hellenization,[9] but the group known as Zealots then emerged and led the revolts against Rome. One may presume that they too had their Syrian counterparts, less well known and perhaps less active. However, it should be noted that some scholars interpret the numerous heresies, such as the Jacobite and Nestorian, that arose during the first few centuries as a nativist reaction against the large Hellenic elements in Christianity. By 132 A.D. the Zealots had been totally crushed, the Jews dispersed, and the victory of Rome and Hellenism seemed finally assured. But then, in 634–636 A.D., came the Arab conquest, which can be interpreted as the final, successful, and definitive Semitic reaction against the Greek intrusion and Hellenistic culture. The place names of Syria are an eloquent witness to the eradication of Hellenism: Halab (Aleppo), for 1,000 years of Greek and Roman domination known as Beroea, reverted to its ancient Semitic name, which it still bears; Palmyra once more became Tadmor, Philadelphia Amman, Heliopolis Baalbeck, Byblos Jebail, and so on. This seems to indicate that the people around them had never stopped using their old Semitic names and is one more indication of how the rural population—who must have constituted well over 80 percent of the total, and perhaps a large chunk of the urban population as well—had been very little affected by Hellenism. Some may indeed have been affected adversely, since Hellenism may have further widened the gulf between them and their Greek, Roman, or Hellenized ruling classes. At the Arab conquest, very large numbers of Greeks left Syria for Constantinople. The Greek defeat seemed complete, but, as we shall see, that was not the end of the story.

The modern European intrusion probably gave an even deeper shock to the Near East than did the Greek. While the world of Islam had been stagnating, Europe had overtaken it in many vitally important fields: technology, science, economic organization, and so on. But militarily the Ottoman Empire held its own until the eighteenth century, and it was not until Bonaparte in Egypt and the future Duke of Wellington in India that European armies overwhelmed Muslim forces in their own lands. By the 1830s the Russians had crushed the Iranians twice, subjugated the Caucasus and TransCaucasia, and repeatedly defeated the Turks. The French had conquered Algeria, the British had established themselves in the Gulf and Aden, and Greece and Serbia had won their independence. In 1840 a small British force captured Acre—the town that had resisted Bona-parte—from Ibrahim pasha, the son of Muhammad Ali.

The following despatch from the British consul in Erzerum, James Brant, to Lord Palmerston, dated 15 April 1841 (FO 78/443), gives a vivid picture of the impact of these events:

> I have the honor to inform your Lordship, that I learned from the Russian Consul-General Khodsko that when the capture of Acre was first reported in Persia, it was scarcely believed by the Shah, but he sent to request the Russian Envoy to come to him. His Majesty told the Envoy he had a question to ask him, and he besought him to an-swer it with candour, as a friend would do to a friend, laying aside the characters of Shah and Envoy. The Envoy promised to reply as de-sired, His Majesty then enquired whether Acre was taken as was re-ported, whether it resisted only a few hours, whether Ibrahim Pasha had been beaten and forced to retire to the Interior, and how many European troops were employed. His Excellency stated that Acre had fallen after a short resistance, that Ibrahim Pasha had retired to Da-mascus, and most of his troops after being beaten deserted him, and that the British landed 1,000 men and the Austrians 200. The replies of the Russian Envoy made a deep and painful impression on the Shah, who became pensive and scarcely spoke again.

> His Majesty like many other persons in these countries, had con-sidered Ibrahim Pasha invincible, and regarded him as the last pillar of Islamism, to find therefore his opinions and hopes falsified occa-sioned him great pain, and perhaps disposed him to believe that since the last support of the Mohamedan faith had failed, the downfall of Islam was not distant.

Once again, as pointed out by Toynbee, the Near East reaction took the twin forms of Zealotism and Herodianism. The Zealots were the Wahhabis in Arabia, Mahdists in Sudan, Sanusis in Libya, and so on; their efforts were crushed by European or European-trained armies. The Herodians were what are now called the "Defen-sive Modernizers," the men who realized that to fight the West re-quired the taking over of many Western ways—not only in military and naval matters but in economics, administration, and education at the very least. Among the Herodians mentioned by Toynbee are Muhammad Ali and Sultan Selim III and Sultan Mahmud II; to them most scholars would add Ismail of Egypt, Abd al-Hamid of Turkey, and Ahmad Bey and Khaireddin of Tunisia.[10]

Neither the early Zealots nor the early modernizers were able to stem the onrushing Western civilization, and more recently we have seen a new phenomenon, what we may call the neo-Herodians and neo-Zealots. Good examples of the former are Mustafa Kemal of Turkey and the late Shah of Iran. Both were staunch patriots, deeply convinced of the excellence of their peoples and the glory of their heritage. But both were equally sure that salvation could come only by the wholesale adoption of Western ways and both were convinced that Islam had burdened their countries and made them retrogress. Among Arabs such attitudes are very rare, with one important exception, the Christians, mostly Lebanese. Many of them have gone to European, mainly French, schools, have deeply assimilated Western culture, and consider themselves part of the West. Indeed many have made a noteworthy contribution to Western literature, like Jibran Khalil Jibran in this country and Andrée Chédid and Georges Schehadé in France, or to science like Sir Peter Medawar, the Nobel laureate, and Sir Michael Atiyah, the mathematician Master of Trinity College, Cambridge, in England. However, in their different ways, the Wafd Party, Gamal Abdel Nasser, and Anwar Sadat should also be included among the Westernizers, even though none of them sought to break violently with their Arab and Islamic past. One could add to this list the numerous and increasingly influential Marxists from all over the Middle East, since they have subscribed to a Western ideology and seek to transform their societies in the image of the West. However, one should note the increasing tendency of Near Eastern Marxists to stress the themes of nationalism and Islam in order to gain mass support.

Countering the neo-Herodians we now have the neo-Zealots, or Islamic fundamentalists, or, more accurately, revivalists. These are very diverse—Shiis and Sunnis, Pakistanis, Iranians, Arabs, Algerians, Turks and so on—but they have two important things in common, their motivation and their ideology.

As for their motivation, its roots are to be found in resentment and frustration, but also, in idealism and a desire for social justice. The resentment springs from many sources, economic, political, and social.

First the political. Unlike Christianity, Islam did not serve a long apprenticeship of oppression and persecution. Almost from the beginning it was triumphant, and its rapid spread within a few decades from Spain to Central Asia was nothing short of miraculous. It could afford to, and did, look down on other cultures and took its supremacy for granted. It successfully dealt with the only two serious threats it encountered in over a thousand years, the Crusades and the Mongol invasion, the first by expulsion, the second by repulsion and conversion. Its only significant losses were Spain and Sicily, beautiful and lamented provinces but both far removed from its heartlands. The Ottoman conquests in Europe gave it a further period of heady triumphs. The ensuing collapse, in the nineteenth century, was therefore even more painful and humiliating than such events inevitably are. And the bitter memories do not seem to have been erased by the achievement of independence and the departure of all the imperial powers, including now the Russians, in the last 50 years or so. Indeed, more than ever, there is the feeling of having been left behind by the course of history.

In the economic field, the incorporation of the Near East into the world market started a process of growth that has resulted in a vast increase in the region's income.[11] But this process, while undoubtedly beneficial in the long run, had two flaws that discredited it in the eyes of the Muslims of the region. First it was, as elsewhere, highly disruptive of old ways and institutions, of guilds and crafts and village communities and established commercial networks. Second, the distribution of the gains made from development was very uneven; by far the largest part of the fruits accrued either to Europeans or to local minority groups: Greeks, Armenians, Jews, Christian Lebanese, and Syrians. Only a very thin layer of Muslims benefited significantly. The rest could not but feel cheated, and this sense still persists, well after all the local sources of wealth have been retaken by the Muslim majority and the Europeans and minorities have departed. The Egyptians still remember the cost to them of the Suez Canal; the Iranians and Iraqis the vast amount of oil shipped out before they began, in the 1950s, to get a large share of the proceeds; the Turks still get indignant over the Public Debt Administration; and the Pakistanis have not forgotten the vast sums drained out of India.

No less painful was the social and cultural impact of the West. Institutions that had been for centuries—or millennia—revered as divine in origin or hallowed by custom were now subjected to opprobrium. In the eyes of Westerners, polygamy was either highly comical or obscene, usually both. Divorce was strongly condemned—that was before the West discovered its attractions. Muslim punishments were now denounced as barbarous. And so on. And it was no consolation to Near Easterners to learn that other great civilizations, like the Chinese and Indian, were regarded with equal contempt by the West, or indeed that Southern and Eastern Europeans did not, in the current scale, rank very much higher.[12]

Resentments can be effaced by success and achievements, but in recent years the Near Easterners have not felt successful and have not been able to achieve their objectives, which are as inconsistent and unrealistic as those of other peoples, advanced or underdeveloped. In spite of independence, they feel that they are still being manipulated by the Powers and defeated by their enemies, India and Israel in particular. Economically, they are as dependent as ever on the industrialized countries, and even the possession of enormous oil resources and financial assets has not provided as much power as it originally promised; to this may be added that oil wealth generated severe economic and social dislocations that have shattered Iran and will probably have the same effect elsewhere. And the onrush of Western mores, carried by a vastly increased number of channels such as television, films, radio, and magazines, seems to pose a mortal threat to Muslim values and morality, particularly in the realm of family life.

Political convulsions have disposed of successive generations of Near Eastern rulers, none of whom has been able to cope with the region's problems. Monarchs were succeeded by civilian rulers, who have been overthrown by military juntas. Nationalist or socialist programs, or amalgams of both, have been tried, but none seems to have made a dent on the numerous ills from which society suffers. Many people feel the need for a new approach. Some look leftward toward communism or some variety of revolutionary Marxism. Others, as in so many parts of the world, including significant groups in the United States, are turning toward religious fundamentalism. The earliest such group was that of the Muslim Brotherhood, founded in Egypt in 1928; it played an active part in the violence that shook Egypt in the 1940s and 1950s and still has a large following. In Syria it is still the most redoubtable opponent of the Alawi-dominated government, and both sides have inflicted terrible blows on each other. But in Egypt it has been eclipsed by far more radical, though much smaller, groups such as that of Denunciation of Unbelief and Call to Holy Flight (*Jama'at al-takfir wal hijra*).

Before examining the ideology of the contemporary Revivalists, it is worthwhile looking at their social composition. Fortunately, we have an in-depth study of 34 militants carried out in the Egyptian jails over a period of two years by a team of Egyptian sociologists led by Saad el-Din Ibrahim, whose results may be summarized as follows.[13] The militants were young, in their early twenties, when they joined the movement. They came from small towns and villages and were recent arrivals in big cities when they were recruited. The vast majority came from the middle class, their fathers being middle-level civil servants, professionals, or small merchants. Most came from "normal cohesive families, i.e., families with no divorce, no separation, no death of either parent." Some 85 percent were university graduates or students; of these, a large majority had taken their degrees in medicine, engineering, and agronomy, that is, in those branches that enjoy most prestige in Egypt, are most highly paid, and attract the best students. Those who had graduated were doing well in their jobs. The scientific training of the militants has attracted much comment in Egypt. Their supporters claim that it is natural: Islam is a religion of reason and therefore attracts those who have been trained in rigorous thinking. Their opponents say that scientists and engineers are narrow in their vision and attracted by simple-minded solutions.

Now let us look at the common features of the ideologies of the various groups. First of all, their unit of reference is not the nation but the whole Islamic community, the *umma*, with its many hundreds of millions stretching from the Philippines to West Africa. Nationalism—in its Arab, Iranian, Turkish, Egyptian, or other forms—is strongly condemned as a modern manifestation of pre-Islamic ignorance (*jahiliya*); probably rightly, it is regarded as one of the many evil ideas picked up from the West.

The *umma* is not only one community, it is the one called by God to lead the world; as the Quran puts it, "You are the best *umma* brought forth for humanity, commanding what is good and forbidding what is evil" (3:10). This is because, of all faiths, Islam is the only one that proclaims, clearly and unequivocally, the *tawhid*, or Unity of God. Moreover, it draws the consequences: faith in God means that *all* aspects of individual and social life must be subordinated to the quest for salvation and must be regulated in accordance with the Divine Law, the *sharia*, not with man-made rules; there is no separation between the realms of Caesar and God. Men imbued with a vibrant belief in *tawhid*, and confident that they are carrying out God's will, are more than a match for many times their number of infidel hedonists, rendered timorous by the fears and greeds that oppress and obsess them. Did not the Arabs demonstrate this when fired by Islam in the seventh century, the Turks in the fifteenth, and the Moghuls in the sixteenth? The infidels include all the polytheists: the Chinese, Indians, and others who are not People of the Book (i.e., who do not have a revealed religion recognized by Islam). The revealed religions are, of course, Judaism and Christianity, whose prophets—Abraham, Moses, Jesus, and others—are revered by Muslims. But since both faiths corrupted the original message given to them by God, they have been superseded by Islam. They have their place in the Islamic society, but a definitely subordinate one. However, today both Christianity and Judaism, operating through colonialism and Zionism, respectively, pose a deep threat to Islam. But the matter goes beyond politics. As the Egyptian revivalist Sayyid Qutb, who was executed by Nasser in 1966 for subversive activities, put it: "[T]he true goal of the People of the Book, whether Jewish or Christian . . . is to lead Muslims astray from their religion to the religion of the People of the Book." This means that Muslims should always be on their guard, but instead they admire Western civilization, accept its norms, and even judge themselves by its standards. To resume the quote:

> It behooves us today to hear this voice of warning, as with unprecedented stupidity we seek the opinions of the Orientalists (of Jews, Christians and unbelieving communists) in the matters of our religion. We learn our history from them, trusting their statements about our heritage, hearing what they interpolate of doubts in their studies of our Qur'an, the *hadith* of our prophet and the lives of our pioneers. We send them delegations of our students to study from them the teachings of Islam. They graduate from their universities and return to us diseased (literally, obsessed by alien forces) in intellect and conscience.[14]

This brings us to the heart of the matter, the Muslim revulsion against Western civilization, in both its capitalist and communist forms. All the Islamic revivalist thinkers, from Pakistan to North Africa, agree in condemning what the Iranian Al-e Ahmad called *gharbzadegi* (i.e., intoxication with the West). Marxism has much appeal to Muslim fundamentalists because it provides a comprehensive ideology, emphasizes the community against the individual, champions the oppressed, and stresses the need for social justice; it even attracted the Muslim Indian poet and philosopher Muhammad Iqbal. But in the final analysis, they reject it too because, in the words of another very influential Iranian, Ali Shariati, it is itself a religion bent "on the systematic eradication of all forms of religion." Moreover, it has its own contradictions. Again, to quote Shariati, Marxism, "whose most basic premise is the denial of the personality in history," has become "the major breeding ground of personality," as the means of its variants indicate: Marxism, Leninism, Trotskyism, Titoism, Maoism, and so on.[15] Needless to say, the Soviet Union's invasion of Afghanistan did not endear it to revivalist Muslims, many of whom gave much help to the Afghan resistance.

Capitalism has far fewer virtues and many more vices. It is essentially based on greed and fear, two sins that are incompatible with a true faith in God. It grinds down the masses and allows the rich to indulge in ostentatious consumption, presenting a corrupting example to the rest of the world. It exploits the bulk of humanity, including more particularly the Muslim world, which it has robbed of oil and other riches. It is arrogant and hegemonic in its attitude to other cultures and often indulges in open racism. Its private values are as bad as its public. Its indulgence in alcohol and heedless mixing of the sexes, and the resulting promiscuity, are deeply offensive to Muslims, who see their youths being seduced by the appeal of those meretricious Western ways. Lastly, even those who admit that the capitalist-liberal model has had some success in Europe and North America would strongly claim that it is inapplicable to the Muslim world—or the Third World in general—and has few or no lessons for them outside the technical and scientific.

For, it should be emphasized, the revivalists do not reject either technology or the natural sciences; only rarely does one see an attack like that of the radical Persian writer Al-e Ahmad on *mashinzadegi*, or intoxication with the machine. It is the Western social sciences that they regard, perhaps rightly, as culture-bound and infirm, and the humanities as outright pagan and dangerous. It is hardly necessary to add that attempts to Westernize Muslim countries, such as Turkey and Iran, are condemned as failures on both the material and moral planes. I am paraphrasing a distinguished Pakistani economist.[16]

What are the lineaments of the Muslim polity that can be discerned in the writings of the leading revivalists? First, they all stress that they are future-oriented: they are trying to build a new society, not to put the clock back as alleged by their enemies. They aim at a theocracy, or rule by God, not one by priests; most of them are very critical of the Muslim religious establishments, which they regard as too subservient to the present godless rulers—whether Saddam Husain of Iraq, Hafiz Asad of Syria, Hosni Mubarak of Egypt, or the rulers of Turkey and Pakistan. However, it is worth noting that in the only successful Islamic revolution to date, that of Iran, power has in fact passed to the *mullahs*, but it should also be noted that Iran is a Shii country where the mullahs have always played a leading part. In the new society, all laws must conform to the *sharia*, or Muslim holy law, and appropriate mechanisms must be set up to ensure that this is done, as in Pakistan and Iran. The courts must also base their judgments on *sharia*. The state thus established must be a populist one. Again and again it is stressed that *all* Muslims—or at the least all men—should participate in the political process through consultation (*shura*) or other means. At the same time most revivalists stress the need to follow a leader, or Guide, who is versed in the Islamic sciences and can provide spiritual and political direction. Once more one can point out that, in Iran, Khomeini's leadership was uncontested and in Libya Qaddafi's—though many Muslims think that Qaddafi has been rather cavalier in his interpretation of Islam.

What about the economic sphere? Khomeini is alleged to have said that economics is for donkeys,[17] which is perhaps slightly exaggerated. Other thinkers have, however, spelled out more fully the economic implications. Let me quote Sadiq al-Mahdi, graduate of Oxford and former prime minister of the Sudan:

> The Economic Sphere: There is no particular Islamic economic system. Islamic economic injunctions require the fulfillment of two conditions: first, the application of certain general principles—for example, that wealth is collectively owned by mankind as vicegerent (representative) of God, that individual ownership is legitimate through effort, that it is a duty to develop and exploit natural resources, that society should provide for the needs of the poor and disabled and so on; second, the establishment of particular injunctions—for example, *zakat* (alms tax), inheritance regulations, and prohibition of usury and indeed prohibition of all unearned income—that obtained through gambling, frauds, the monopoly of profits, and so on. Abiding by those two conditions, contemporary Islamic economic thinking may study modern economic theories and institutions, inform itself of current economic needs, and design an economic system which is both Islamic and modern and which will be able to effect economic development as well as an equitable distribution of its outcome.[18]

It should be added that considerable ingenuity has been shown in devising means to obey the injunction against usury by forbidding interest but allowing profit-sharing.[19] One should also mention the Islamic Development Fund which, between 1972 and 1982, advanced $3 billion, of which $1 billion was for projects and the rest for financing foreign trade.

As for the position of women, there is a fairly wide consensus. Women should dress "decently" (i.e., cover all their body except the face and hands). They should receive education (how much is a matter of controversy: some say as much as men, other much less) but, on the whole, be restricted to the professions for which they are particularly fitted, for example, medicine, nursing, teaching, etc. They should enjoy voting and other political rights but are not expected to take a leading part in politics. Of course, as in the past, they may own property and inherit their prescribed shares, which are smaller than those of men.

Now comes the last question: what are the prospects of these movements? Will the Islamic *umma* achieve the leadership it believes to be its due? This looks unlikely when one considers the giants hemming it on every side: China, India, and Russia—all of which have large Muslim minorities—and the West, which no longer rules over Muslim lands. But it is worth remembering Arnold Toynbee's warning, made nearly 40 years ago, that, in case of a world explosion, "Islam might have quite a different part to play as the active ingredient in some violent reaction of the cosmopolitan under-world against its Western masters." And again, "If the present situation of mankind were to precipitate a 'race war,' Islam might be moved to play her historical role once again. *Absit omen.*"[20]

But if we leave such macrocosmic speculations aside and look at the future of the Near East, we have to ask whether the Muslim revivalist wave will sweep over the region. The answer is that it very well may, even though there are strong local forces bitterly opposed to it. In other words, in the present encounter between the Near East and the West, as in the previous one between it and Greco-Roman civilization, the Zealots may well be victorious and the Herodians swept away. But that is not the end of the story.

First, the past. Although the Zealots won, Greek culture bore rich fruits in the Near East. First and foremost, it produced Christianity, a faith rejected by the Near East but which went on to convert and civilize new peoples who became the standard bearers of the most dynamic culture the world has seen. Jesus came from "Galilee of the Gentiles." St. Luke wrote his Gospel in Greek. The Gospel according to St. John is a very Hellenic work. St. Paul was a strict and devout Jew (in his own words: "Of the people of Israel, of the tribe of Benjamin, a Hebrew born of Hebrews, as to the law a Pharisee"— Philippians I, 3,), but it was in Greek that he thought and preached his message to the Gentiles, and he—and his audience—knew and used the Greek translation of the Old Testament known as the Septuagint.[21]

And Hellenism also permeated the Muslim Near East, shaping its science and philosophy and deeply marking its theology. Perhaps after all, the Zealots did not win.

The Western impact on the Near East has been broader and deeper than the Greek ever was. At the mass level it has permeated the lives of millions of people through technology, economic relations, and mass media. And among the educated classes Western science, philosophy, literature, scholarship, the arts, and Western mores have struck deep roots. No one can foresee which Western elements will be retained and which rejected, but one can be confident that, in any future synthesis or amalgam, the Western contribution will be prominent.

Notes

Lecture given to Princeton alumni, in October 1986, with the same title.

1. Michael Grant, *From Alexander to Cleopatra* (New York, 1982), p. 61.

2. Ibid., p. 69.

3. Ibid., p. 63.

4. Ibid., p. 58.

5. Arnold Toynbee: "Islam, the West and the Future," *Civilization on Trial* (New York, 1948), pp. 188, 193.

6. F. E. Peters, *The Harvest of Hellenism* (New York, 1970), p. 302.

7. Arnaldo Momigliano, *Alien Wisdom: The Limits of Hellenism* (Cambridge, 1975), p. 88.

8. Peters, op. cit., p. 548.

9. Ibid., p. 291.

10. It is worth noting that Ernest Renan draws a parallelism between the way in which Herod and Ismail pasha introduced Hellenism and Europeanism into their respective countries. See *Histoire du Peuple d'Israel, Oeuvres Complètes,* vol. 6, pp. 1, 420. I owe this reference to Dr. Henry Laurens, of the Sorbonne.

11. See Charles Issawi, *An Economic History of the Middle East and North Africa* (New York, 1982).

12. That acute student, and eminent practitioner, of imperialism, Lord Cromer, was keenly aware of the revulsion of Muslims at many aspects of Western civilization and their increased conviction of the superiority of Islam. This led him to conclude that modern European imperialism (British, French, Dutch, and Russian) would prove to be more ephemeral than Ro-

man. See Earl of Cromer, *Ancient and Modern Imperialism* (New York, 1910).

13. Saad Eddin Ibrahim, "Anatomy of Egypt's Militant Islamic Groups," *International Journal of Middle Eastern Studies*, November 1980. The most thorough and comprehensive study of the Egyptian Muslim revivalists is Gilles Keppel, *Le Prophète et le Pharaon* (Paris, 1982). The English translation is *The Prophet and Pharaoh* (London, 1983).

14. Yvonne Yazbeck Haddad, "The Quranic Justification for an Islamic Revolution," *Middle East Journal*, Winter 1983.

15. Brad Hanson, "The Westoxication of Iran," *International Journal of Middle Eastern Studies*, February 1983.

16. Khurshid Ahmad, "The Islamic Approach to Economic Development," in John L. Esposito (ed.), *Voices of Resurgent Islam* (New York, 1983), p. 224.

17. Michael Fischer, "Imam Khomeini: Four Levels of Understanding," in Esposito, op. cit., p. 169.

18. Al-Sadiq al-Mahdi, "Islam—Society and Change," in Esposito, op. cit., p. 237.

19. See Charles Issawi, "The Adaptation of Islam to Contemporary Economic Realities"; idem, *The Middle East Economy: Decline and Recovery* (Princeton, 1995), pp. 187–206.

20. Op. cit., pp. 209, 212.

21. Peters, op. cit., p. 299.

TWO

EMPIRE BUILDERS, CULTURE MAKERS,
AND CULTURE IMPRINTERS

Surveying the world today, we see several huge areas in which hundreds of millions of people share a religion, laws, institutions, arts, architecture, cooking, and a way of life. Apart from physical differences, the outward characteristic which distinguishes these regions from each other is a language. They are the Chinese, Indian (notwithstanding the presence of many large linguistic groups), Anglo-Saxon, Russian (not including the Caucasus and Central Asia), Latin American, Latin European, and Arab culture areas; the last consists of an Arab mass and a small linguistic fringe in east and west Africa.[1] Together, they account for about two thirds of the world population. The two most populous regions, the Chinese and Indian, were formed some centuries before the Christian era and the Latin European—Italy, France, Spain, Portugal, and parts of Belgium and Switzerland—during the Roman domination; although Rumania belongs linguistically to the Romance group, historically, religiously, and legally it does not. The Arab area was formed during the first few centuries of the Muslim era (that is, starting in 622, the year of the Hijra, or flight) and the Anglo-Saxon, Latin American, and Russian regions in the last 500 or 600 years.

This list raises some intersting questions. Why did the Romans and not the Greeks found such a culutral area? Why the Arabs and not the Persians? Why the Spaniards and not the French? Why the Russians and not the Germans? In every case it was the culturally less creative people that imprinted a large area. Was this achievement because they were more successful as empire builders; that is, they showed greater political and military skill? These factors were certainly important, but they do not exhaust the question. A full study of empire builders and culture makers is needed before we can address the central topic: what enabled certain peoples and not others, to imprint ther languatge and culture over a vast area.

EMPIRE BUILDERS

Which of the innumberable states in world history should be regarded as empires and included in this study? Empires are characterized by a diversity of peoples dominated by one of them, a vast extent of territory, a large population, and durability over time. For our purposes an arbitrary but reasonable figure of about 1 million square miles (an area slightly larger than that of the European Community and over a quarter that of the Unites States) will be taken as the minimum area and 200 years as the minimum duration.

No similar figure can be suggested for population, since the totals varied significantly over the long period studied in this chapter. Both the Roman Empire and the Han Empire at the beginning of the Christian era had an estimated population of 60 million. The Omayyad Empire, at the fall of the dynasty in 750, may have had some 30 million, and a similar figure has been suggested for the Seleucid Empire in the third century B.C. The Byzantine population in the year 1000 A.D. may have been 15 to 20 million, and the Ottoman population at the end of the sixteenth century may, with some confidence, be set at 30 to 35 million. The populations of the Portuguese and Spanish empires were smaller: as late as 1750, the total number of inhabitants of South and Central America was only 16 million and, in 1800, 24 million. The Dutch Empire had a comparable population until the upsurge of the nineteenth century. The Austro-Hungarian Empire had some 50 million inhabitants at the outbreak of World War. I. The modern empires, such as the British, French, Russian, and Chinese, have had populations of 100 million or more, as did the Mongol Empire in the period when it included China and the Near East. The other ancient and medieval empires mentioned in this chapter had populations of a few million, or even less; for example, even at its height, the Venetian Empire cannot have had more than a million or so inhabitants. Population estimates for India are highly conjectural, but both the Maurya and the Gupta empires may have had over 10 million inhabitants, and the Moghul Empire's population in 1600 has been estimated at 100 million.[2]

My review of the various empires that have flourished in the last 4,000 years has eliminated some from further discussion because they were too small, some because they lasted too brief a time, and some because they were both too small and too short-lived. Those that were extensive but lasted less than 200 years include the Maurya (324?–183 B.C.), Gupta (320–500? A.D.), Mongol (1206–1349), and Timurid (1369–1469) empires, the second French Empire (1815–1960), and the Japanese Empire (1873–1945). Among the empires that lasted over 200 years but were too small to qualify are the Akkadian, Egyptian, Carthaginian, Venetian, Byzantine, Swedish, and Austro-Hungarian empires. Those that were both too short-lived and too small include the Hittite, Neo-Babylonian, and Athenian among ancient empires, and the Italian and German among modern ones.

Despite these exclusions, there is still a long list to be examined. Among ancient empires there are the Assyrian, Seleucid, and Roman, and the Achaemenian, Parthian, and Sassanian empires of Persia.[3] Most important in medieval times is the Arab Empire. It includes the Omayyad and early Abbasid empires, from about 640 to the 860s A.D., when—following the earlier loss of Spain and North Africa—the Tulunids in Egypt and the Saffarids in Iran shook off the rule of the caliphate. Modern empires include the Ottoman, Moghul, Portuguese, Spanish, Dutch, British, and Russian. And straddling all of these periods stands the Chinese Empire.

In order to decrease the degree of arbitrariness in the criteria selected, one can reduce the figures given above. Bringing down the minimum age limit to, say, 100 years would add the two Indian and the French and Mongol empires to the list. Reducing the size drastically would add the Hittite, Neo-Babylonian, and Byzantine empires. Except for the Maurya, none of these empires can be considered a culture imprinter as defined later in this chapter.

No attempt is made to study the factors that facilitated the establishment and expansion of empires. This decision means omitting all reference to military, economic, demographic, technological, and other aspects of history which, although of the utmost importance in other respects, are not essential to the point at issue: the reasons for the formation of culture areas. With few exceptions, no attempt is made to discuss ideologies of empire.

CULTURE MAKERS

In this section, culture is interpreted in a very restricted sense; it refers only to "high culture," that is, religion, law, literature, philosophy, the natural and human sciences, music, and the visual arts. Even within these limits, the number of peoples who have made valuable contributions is very large. Moreover, it is impossible to suggest the kinds of precise—if somewhat arbitrary—criteria for inclusion and exclusion used in the previous section.

However, a beginning may be made by listing some of the peoples whose claims to have made a great contribution would be generally recognized: the Sumerians, Egyptians, Babylonians, Greeks, Jews, Indians, Chinese, Mayas, Persians (ancient and medieval), Italians, French, British (with their American offshoot), and Germans (including the Austrians). All of these peoples made significant contributions to most of the fields listed in the preceding paragraph. Four additional groups require more extended discussion: the Romans, Arabs, Spaniards, and Russians. Many scholars claim that Roman culture was derivative and added little to what it had taken over from Greece; others, by contrast, claim that the Roman (including, in some fields, Italian—the distinction had become meaningless by the first century B.C.) contribution to politics, law, literature, and architecture is sufficient to warrant inclusion.

Some scholars maintain that the Arabs, too, made a limited contribution to the culture of the Islamic civilization. A breakdown of the leading translators, philosophers, physicians, mathematicians, astronomers, physicists, chemists, historians, geographers, and grammarians in the medieval Muslim Middle East shows the overwhelming majority to have been non-Arabs who wrote in Arabic. Of these, the Persians were by far the most important group. In a chapter of *Al-Muqaddima* entitled "Most of the Learned Men in Islam Have Been Non-Arabs (Persians)," Ibn Khaldun gives a penetrating sociological explanation of this phenomenon. He argues that learning can develop only in a sedentary society, where the crafts enjoy a long and uninterrupted tradition and receive much attention. Hence, the Arabs could not be expected to produce any learning so long as they remained nomads. "Those Arabs, however, who forsook a nomadic for a sedentary life concentrated all their energies on politics, rulership and war. This bred a disdain for the pursuit of learning as a profession, since it had become one of the crafts; for the ruling classes always look down on the crafts and professions and all that pertains to them." Thus, learning and scholarship were left to the non-Arab sedentary populations, such as "the Persians, or those who were politically and culturally subject to them and who had, therefore, developed a skill in the sciences and crafts owing to a long tradition of civilization." However, in addition to providing the religion and language which formed the foundation of Islam, the Arabs, like the Romans, who constituted a similar ruling group, excelled in law, poetry, and philology.[4]

As for Spain, in its Golden Century, it was second to none in literature and painting. Since then, it has made important contributions to painting and music. Although these achievements do not place Spain in the first rank, they may entitle it to inclusion among the culture makers.

The Russian case is also doubtful: Russia's cultural contribution is concentrated in about 100 years—from the 1820s to the 1920s—and in two fields, literature and music, including ballet. But the brilliance of that contribution may be regarded as offsetting its narrowness and short duration.

Among the peoples that have been left out are some whose claim is strong: the Byzantines with their scholarship, architecture, and painting; the Ottomans with their architecture; the Dutch with their science and painting; the Japanese with their woodcuts; and so on. But their inclusion would not significantly affect the conclusions drawn in this study.

CULTURE IMPRINTERS

Culture imprinters are those peoples who have stamped several elements of both their high and their popular cultures on a large number of persons inhabiting a big area. Among these elements are language, religion, laws, architecture, cuisine, some institutions and ways of life, and certain types of folk music and art. In contrast to the section on culture makers, where culture referred only to high culture, here we are dealing with the culture of masses.

Most empires, including some of the largest and some of the longest lived, failed to leave a lasting imprint of their culture over a large area. The culture of the ancient empires (Babylonian, Egyptian, and Carthaginian) was overlaid by that of Greece and Rome and was finally dissolved and absorbed by Christianity and Islam.

The pre-Islamic Persian empires (Achaemenian, Parthian, and Sassanian) left little imprint outside Iran, and the same is true of the Ottomans outside Turkey. The Mongol Empire vanished with little trace and so did the Byzantine in its Asian areas, although it deeply influenced eastern Europe through its religion, art, and script. It can be safely predicted that the modern empires will leave little permanent imprint in Asia or Africa, except for technology and religion in some countries: this statement applies both to the European empires (Portuguese, Spanish, Dutch, French, British, Belgian, Italian, and German) and to the Japanese. The impact of the Austro-Hungarian Empire on the culture of its non-Germanic peoples was not great—it did not change the language and religion of the people.

Most of the ethnic groups with very brilliant and active cultures failed to leave a cultural imprint over a large area. Examples include the Italians, French, and Germans in modern times and the Jews, Greeks, and Persians in ancient times. Nor does the degree of "openness" or "universality" of a culture seem to have much effect on whether or not it will be imprinted. Thus, it has been repeatedly stated by Frenchmen, and generally accepted by Continental Europeans, that French culture had a more universal aspect than English or Spanish or Russian and was couched in terms that could more easily be understood and adopted by foreigners; and, in fact, it was so adopted by Europe's aristocracy. But French culture has not left on the map of the world the kind of imprint that the English or Spanish or Russian has; there are no large regions where French is the mother tongue.

By contrast, most of the culture makers provided the "classical" language of the civilization in which they lived, that is, the language of learning. Examples are Chinese, Sanskrit, Greek and Latin in the Roman Empire, Arabic in medieval Islam, Latin in medieval Europe, Persian in what Arnold Toynbee has called the Iranic Society, stretching from Turkey to cental India and Central Asia from the fifteenth to the nineteenth centuries, and, for some centuries, French in modern Europe; American English seems to be emerging as the classical language of the world civilization that is slowly being formed today.[5]

Three conditions have favored cultural imprinting. First, the existence of an empire which provided the framework within which the culture could spread; this fact has been true in all of the instances mentioned earlier: Chinese, Indian, Roman, Arab, Portuguese (in Brazil), Spanish, British, and Russian. Second, it has required the migration of fairly—or very—large numbers of the culture bearers from the core to the outlying parts; they included all sorts of people, from priests and scholars to ruffians and convicts. This statement also applies to all of the culture areas with the possible exception of the Indian, about which little is known. In the Chinese, Russian, Latin American, and Anglo-Saxon areas, such migration ran into the millions; in the Roman and Arab areas, it was probably in the hundreds of thousands. Third, in most cases, the culture either was, or soon came to be, identified with a religion that either actively proselytized or at least easily admitted converts; this was certainly true of all of the Christian, Muslim, and Indian empires studied here. Such a religion had a threefold effect on cultural imprinting. First, it established the rulers' language as a sacred language, superior to all others. Second, it helped to spread the culture among the masses, as distinct from the small upper-class and urban layers on whom imperial rulers relied and who were often influenced by the rulers' culture. Third, it helped society to withstand such shocks as the invasions of the barbarians in the Western Roman Empire or the Mongols and Turks in the Arab and Persian heartlands, by preserving the imprinted culture and eventually converting the conquerors.

The success of the Romans, as contrasted with the failure of the Greeks and the Europeans in Asia and Africa, is instructive. The main reason why Rome Latinized the western Mediterranean, whereas Greece did not Hellenize the eastern Mediterranean, is that Rome was dealing with relatively primitive peoples and Greece with highly civilized ones, strongly tenacious of their old cultures. In Syria, for instance, Greek culture, with all its brilliance, attracted only a small layer of upper- or middle-class urban people.[6] Some Syrians wholeheartedly assimilated Hellenism, adopted Greek names, and even contributed to Greek literature, philosophy, and science; examples include the philosophers Zeno and Posidonius, the poet Meleager, the writer Lucian, and, in the Roman period, the jurists Ulpian and Papinian, who taught in the law school of Beirut.

The masses, however, seem to have been little affected, and indeed may have strongly resented Hellenism as the badge of an upper class from whom they now felt triply alienated: eonomically, socially, and culturally. An indication of this alienation is the fact that, after having borne Greek names for a thousand years, Beroea, Palmyra, Heliopolis, Philadelphia, and other cities reverted to their ancient Semitic names of Aleppo, Tadmor, Balbeck, Amman, and so forth. This phenomenon suggests that the inhabitants around the cities—

and perhaps many inside them—had never stopped using the old names. However, some newly founded coastal cities, for example, Antioch and Laodicea, as well as the not so ancient one of Tripoli, retained their Greek names—perhaps because the coastal areas were more Hellenized than the interior, although it should be noted that the port of Byblos took back its old Semitic name of Jebeil. In Egypt, Mesopotamia, and Iran, the impact of Hellenism was still more restricted, despite the fact that the Greek *koine* (common tongue) was widely used throughout the eastern Mediterranean.[7]

Another important aspect should be noted: Christianity came to Western Europe in a Latin form, which it ratained until the Reformation. This fact had a twofold effect. First, it presumably facilitated the Romanization of the provinces in the last centuries of the empire; in addition to being the language of administration and culture, Latin became the language of religion and salvation, and the Church was a far more effective propagandist than the State had been. Second, the Church was a powerful factor in preserving the Latin character of Western Europe during the barbarian invasions.

In the Near East, by contrast, national churches, using the vernacular (Coptic, Syriac, and Armenian), arose at a very early date. A good index of this phenomenon is that the earliest translations of at least part of the New Testament into Syriac date from the second century (Aramaic versions of the Old Testament are far older), into Coptic from the third, and into Armenian from the fifth century. The existence of these churches, which soon adopted various heresies—Nestorian, Monophysite, Monothelete, and others—greatly strengthened local ethnicities and acted as a strong force opposing Hellenization. Even where the elites retained their knowledge of Greek, the masses practiced religion in their native tongue. Conversely, the earliest Latin version of parts of the New Testament originated in North Africa in the second century, and the fourth century Vulgate was soon adopted in the Western Roman Empire.[8]

In this connection, one may ask why, after the barbarian invasions, the spoken tongue in Gaul remained close to Latin, whereas in Britain one part of the inhabitants (at first by far the majority, and then a steadily shrinking minority) spoke Gaelic languages and the other part Anglo-Saxon. The answer is surely not to be found in demography. The number of Angles, Saxons, and Jutes who came to Britain by ship must have been far smaller than that of the various Germanic tribes (Visigoths, Burgundians, Franks, and others) that marched into Gaul. Moreover, it is generally agreed that the Roman-

ized Britons in the area of Anglo-Saxon settlement around 500—
even after allowance has been made for large losses through emigration, famine, pestilence, and war—"probably outnumer[ed] their invaders many, many times."9

Part of the explanation is that, around 400 A.D., Gaul was more
Latinized than was Britain. Jones argues that "Latin was the only
language of Italy, and probably had ousted Celtic, Ligurian and Iberian in Southern Gaul and in eastern and southern Spain. The survival of Welsh and Cornish implies that Celtic was still the dominant language in Britain when it was lost to the empire in the fifth
century. There is evidence for the survival of Celtic in Gaul at the
same period."10

Archaeological finds since the 1950s suggest that Latin was widespread in Britain, too. According to Morris, "The pens used for writing on wax tablets, called *styli*, are found in numbers in towns, and
are not uncommon in the countryside; they are evidence not only of
literacy but of Latin, for British was unwritten." A breakdown by region and class suggests that Latin was used in the lowlands, the
towns, the army, the government, and the Church, and by the upper
classes, often in addition to British.11

Other reasons why Gaul remained Latin and Britain did not are
to be found in the state of the Church, the fate of the aristocracy,
and the interconnection between the two. In the fourth century, religion had been active enough in Britain "to foster one of the great
early heresiarchs, Pelagius, who left the country about 380." By
the first half of the fifth century, however, the best that could be said
was that there was not a "complete breakdown of the Roman administration and religion." Although Christianity continued to spread in
the Celtic highlands, the Church was greatly weakened, or had dis-
appeared, in the Anglo-Saxon lowlands. Later, when the Church
and learning centered in the Church had developed in Ireland
and Britain, "during the eighth century Latinity went back to Gaul
through Britain." By then, Britain had become irreversibly committed to Anglo-Saxon and Gaelic.12

In Gaul, however, the Church remained very powerful. Mona-
chism had come early and spread widely, and numerous hermits were
to be found in the countryside; by the fifth century, monasteries were
being founded and were receiving generous endowments. Still more
important were the bishops; speaking of this period, one Catholic
historian went so far as to say that "la France est l'oeuvre de ses pre-
miers évêques comme la ruche est l'oeuvre de ses abeilles." Dill was

almost as emphatic: "We may indeed venture to say that never in the long history of the Church of Rome did her bishops wield a greater power than in sixth century Gaul." This power was accompanied by a rapid growth in the wealth of the Church.[13]

One factor that explains the much greater strength of the Church in Gaul than in Britain, apart from its deeper roots and wider base, was its connecton with the aristocracy. Following the barbarian invasions, a very large part of the aristocracy of Britain seems to have migrated to Brittany and elsewhere. In Gaul, by contrast, the majority of the aristocrats stayed, and, even before the invasions, many of them had become bishops.[14]

Similar considerations explain the failure of modern European empires to imprint their culture in a durable form. On the one hand, they too faced mainly very ancient, proud, and tenacious cultures. On the other, they encountered powerful religions—Islam, Hinduism, and Buddhism—which showed no sign of relinquishing their hold on the allegiance of their members. This fact was very clearly perceived by Lord Cromer, a noted student of Roman imperialism and practitioner of British imperialism in India and Egypt. In his *Ancient and Modern Imperialism*, he explained clearly why contemporary European empires—British, French, Dutch, and Russian—would prove less durable and have less impact than the Roman.[15] Moreover, he believed—rightly in my opinion—that, unlike Latin, the European languages (English in India and Egypt, French in North Africa, and Dutch in Indonesia) would eventually be rejected in favor of the local tongues; whether, in Central Asia and the Caucasus, Russian will prevail is, in my opinion, moot.

Cromer argued very convincingly that the Romans "succeeded far better" partly because they had an easier task and partly because they showed greater powers of assimilation. After the overthrow of Egypt in 31 B.C., they did not face any hostile great power except Persia. The religions of their subjects could easily be, and were, assimilated to their own. "It was Christianity and its offshoot, Islam, that created nations and introduced the religious element into politics." In the one case where the Romans encountered "an unassimilative religion [the Jewish] their failure was complete."[16] Egypt is another example of a stubborn nationalism based on a strong religion.

What makes the better preformance of Rome more remarkable is that at least three modern empires—the Spanish, British, and French—thought of themselves as the heirs of Rome and modeled themselves on it. As early as Hernando Cortés, the Spaniards were comparing their conquests with those of Rome. As Cortés reportedly put it, "If God helps us, far more will be said in future history books about our exploits than had ever been said about those of the past."[17]

The French considered it their mission to spread "civilization" (i.e., Latinity) to their subjects. This view is strikingly apparent both in French historiography on North Africa and in France's policy toward that region, especially during the interwar period. In the words of a distinguished French scholar, "Africa was slowly being Latinized. And the descriptions taken up by the analysts of the contemporary period could be used as a link between the Roman conquest and the French conquest. *Ense et aratro,* by the sword and the plough: the slogan took one back to the sources, which made for continuity, transmission, heritage."[18]

The British were less interested in culture and more in Pax Romana; one of the favorite quotations of British students of their empire was:

To spare the vanquished and the proud to tame.
These are imperial arts and worthy of thy name.[19]

Cromer developed at length the analogies between Roman and British imperialism, especially in India: the initial reluctance of part of the public to extend the empire (which was overcome by the push toward defensible frontiers); the use of client states to avoid direct rule; the ambitions of local generals and governors; the pull of dissensions between tribes and statelets; the desire to forestall occupation by another great power (Persia in one case, and France and Russia in the other); the use of military auxiliaries drawn from the subject populations; the initial plunder of colonies, followed by more orderly and humane methods; the baleful effects of unrestrained moneylenders and traders from the metropolis; and the respect for and toleration of local customs and institutions in combination with the abolition of certain cruel practices (for example, Druid worship and *suttee*).[20]

It can be argued that modern imperialism differs from the earlier version and should not be judged by the same criteria. Its aims are essentially economic: to open new sources of raw materials and secure outlets for finished goods and capital. It seeks to impose not culture but institutions that facilitate political control and economic exchange. Its main contributions have been in the realm of technology, science, and institutions, not language and religion. Its influence in these fields is likely to outlast its political control. Moreover, it may be maintained, a new world civilization is being slowly formed; the main characteristics of this new civilization are based on science, technology, and capitalism (or socialism), and its "classical" language is American English.

This argument underrates the power and durability of the old cultures and religions. The extension of technology and exchanges is not preventing Islamic, Hindu, and Buddhist revivalism, which affects large sectors of individual and social life. The world civilization that is emerging will still show deep cultural rifts. Indeed, some observers doubt whether modern science and technology can thrive in a "fundamentalist" Muslim or Hindu society. Muslim revivalists emphatically proclaim that they welcome Western science and technology; it is Western humanism and social science—and Western religion and irreligion—that they reject. And it is interesting to note that most of the leaders of the Muslim groups in Egypt have had a technical or scientific education. It is premature to pass judgment on this question.

The close connection between religion and culture imprinting is also shown by the examples of the Arab and Indian areas. The main reason why the Arab conquerors were able to spread their language and culture over such a large area—in striking contrast to the Goths, Vandals, Franks, and others and to the Mongols a few centuries later—is that they brought with them a religion that found ready acceptance among their subjects. And Islamicization implied Arabization, since, more than in most faiths, religion and language are inseparable. Furthermore, like almost all other religions, Islam carried its own script. In addition, the Islamic Middle East (Arab-Persian) was able to assimilate its barbarian invaders (Turks and Mongols) even more successfully than did Roman Christianity, by rapid conversion. The numerous Turkic slaves who formed much of the region's military aristocracy—for example, under the Abbasids in Iraq from about 850 on and as Mamluk rulers of Egypt from about 1250 to 1517 and later—were converted on arrival and given an Islamic education. The great Turkic dynasties—including the Ghaznavids (976–1186), who ruled eastern Iran, Afghanistan, and northern India; the Saljuks (1055–1117), whose empire stretched from Anatolia to Afghanistan; and the Ottomans (1290–1918)—had become Muslims before they took power. Even the Mongols, at the height of their might and fury, did not resist Islam for long. In 1253, Hulegu set out on his western conquests and in 1258 sacked and utterly destroyed Baghdad. But, by 1295, his great-grandson Ghazan, who ruled the Il-Khan state centered in Iran, converted to Islam and became a noted patron of Islamic learning. A few years earlier, the Mongol ruler of the Golden Horde, centered in the Volga valley, and containing a large Muslim population of Bulghars, had also become a Muslim.[21]

However, although the Turks and Mongols were Islamized, and soon "civilized," they were not Arabized except insofar as Arabic was the religious, legal, and scientific language of Islam. In this respect, they are like the Saxons, Czechs, Hungarians, and Poles, rather than the Franks or Lombards.

The Persians, who preceded the Arabs, and the Ottomans, who succeeded them, present a striking contrast. Both had large and highly civilized empires, and the Ottomans certainly, and the Persians probably, showed much greater aptitude for creating solid political and administrative institutions than did the Arabs. Regarding the Ottomans, the sheer durability of the empire (1290–1918), the continuity of its dynasty, and the enormous volume and high quality of its archives (put at 50 million documents) are proof enough. The Persians were surely not the equals of the Ottomans and have left far less evidence behind them. But the fact that the Arab caliphate, especially under the Abbasids (750–1258), patterned itself closely on the Persian monarchy and took over, with very minor modifications, its fiscal and administrative system—including some of its vocabulary—shows how highly Persian institutions were regarded (indeed, Arab historians and political scientists have always held up the Persian monarchy as a model). But neither the Persians nor the Ottomans succeeded in converting substantial numbers outside thier homeland, and therefore, when their domination ceased, the former provinces kept little trace of the metropolitan culture. The spread of the Persian language and culture throughout the Iranic society did not occur until Iran had been thoroughly Islamized and was greatly facilitated by that religion.[22]

The role of the Orthodox Church in the formation of the Russian cultural area is too well known for elaboration here. Conversion in 987 brought the Kievan state into surprisingly close relations not only with Constantinople but also with Western Europe, as evidenced by marriages, in the middle of the eleventh century, with the royal houses of Sweden, Norway, Poland, Hungary, France, and England. The Church introduced literacy and the arts. It preserved Russian culture under the Mongol yoke and helped to mobilize the

Russians against Polish, Lithuanian, and other invaders. Lastly, it contributed greatly to the elaboration of the Muscovite autocracy.

Similarly, most scholars would agree that the most important single factor holding India together, and enabling it to survive repeated conquests, has been the Hindu religion. Likewise, the conversion to Roman Catholicism of the native populations of Mexico, Peru, and other densely settled areas helped greatly in Hispanizing Central and South America—a process that is by no means complete. It is also possible that Confucianism and Taoism helped China recover its unity after the breakdown of the Han Empire in the third century A.D. and the fragmentation and retrogression caused by the barbarian invasions.

Another factor mentioned by Cromer is the easier social relations prevailing between the Romans and their subjects than between the Europeans and theirs. In fact, he devotes a long appendix to the question of Roman (and Greek) intermarriage with other races and concludes that it was "no uncommon incident." Moreover, his "own conjecture—and it is nothing more than a conjecture—is that antipathy based on differences of color is a plant of comparatively recent growth. It seems probable that it received a great stimulus from the world-discoveries of the fifteenth century. One of the results of these discoveries was to convince the white Christian that he might, not only with profit, but with strict propriety, enslave the black heathen." Syme was of the same opinion: "The Romans evince no sort of preoccupation with racial purity."[23]

Some present-day scholars disagree, maintaining that "the much touted absence of racial prejudice in the Roman Empire is a myth of modern times" and that this prejudice went beyond simple cultural prejudice.[24] But, the degree of intermarriage between Romans and other inhabitants of the Empire seems to have been higher than in some modern empires, a factor that, more than any other, promotes the fusion of peoples. The same was true of the Arabs, who also showed less racial prejudice and—greatly helped by polygamy and the fact that the children of concubines were considered legitimate—intermarried more freely with their subjects than did the Europeans.

In China, as in the Latin American, Anglo-Saxon, and Russian areas, emigration was the major factor in spreading culture. From Han times onward, the Chinese slowly conquered and settled the provinces lying south of the Yangtze River, eventually converting them into the economic center of the empire. In Latin America outside Mexico and the Andes, the Spanish and Portuguese settled almost empty lands and created melting pots into which poured immigrants from many European, African, and Asian countries, who were slowly assimilated. The same was true of the Anglo-Saxons in North America and Australasia. The Russians also spread over a very thinly populated area (European Russia and Siberia), but the populations there remained much more homogeneous and attracted few immigrants from other countries. (Russsian settlement in Muslim Central Asia is likely to have a different outcome.)[25]

Geography has also proved to be an important factor. The main cultural areas generally originated, and spread and established themselves, in lowlands. The reasons are obvious: lowlands can support large populations and facilitate cultural interactions and transmission, particularly when they are crossed by navigable rivers. Chinese civilization was born along the Yellow River and eventually spread to the Yangtze region and beyond. Indian civilization developed in the Indus lowlands and spread to the Gangetic plain. The Latinization of Western Europe was most successful in the plains, whereas the inhabitants of the mountains of Gaul, Spain, and Britain continued to use Celtic or other languages. Russian culture spread in the vast plains, and along the great rivers. In Latin America, such mountainous regions as Mexico, Peru, and Bolivia have been most resistant to Hispanization. Anglo-Saxon culture took shape in the lowlands of Britain and spread most widely in the North American plains. Lastly, as Ibn Khaldun has pointed out, in a chapter enitled "Arabs Conquer Only Plains," Arab culture has also spread mainly in lowlands.[26] The Taurus mountains and plateau of Anatolia and the Zagros mountains and highlands of Iran prevented the Arabization of these regions—but not their Islamization. And substantial pockets of Kurds, Berbers, and other non-Arabs continue to live in the mountainous zones of the Middle East and North Africa.

To conclude, a people's success in culture imprinting bears no direct relationship to its brilliance in "high culture"; the most creative of them all, the Greeks, Italians, French, and Germans and, one is tempted to add, the Persians and Jews, did not imprint their cultures over vast areas. Conversely, most of the culture imprinters—the Romans, Arabs, Portuguese, Spaniards, and Russians—made relatively little contribution to "high culture."

The correlation between a people's capacity to create durable political and administrative institutions and the extent of its cultural imprinting is somewhat closer, but by no means high: some of the most capable imperialists, like the Assyrians, Achaemenid Persians, Ottomans, and Habsburgs, did not leave much imprint, and some of the less capable, like the Indians, Arabs, and Portuguese, did. But an imperial framework was indispensable for the creation of a culture area.

The effect on culture imprinting of two other factors, chronology and form of government, may also be briefly examined. As regards chronology, there seems to be no significant correlation between it and the formation of cultural areas. The Chinese and Indian areas took shape well before the Christian era, the Latin European and Arab areas in late antiquity, and the Latin American, Russian, and Anglo-Saxon in early modern times. Neither the early empires of antiquity—such as the Egyptian, Assyrian, and Persian—nor the modern ones—such as the French, Italian, and German—have imprinted their cultures in a durable manner.

As for forms of government, all of the peoples who imprinted their culture lived under a traditional, more or less autocratic monarchy, governing through the usual ruling classes: the landed aristocracy, army, church, and bureaucracy. Rome had an aristocratic government, which gradually broadened to democracy before reverting to autocratic rule under Julius Caesar and Augustus. Britain, in its imperial period, was a constitutional monarchy, with power gradually extending from the aristocracy to the middle class. But in no case does the form of government of the metropolis make a significant difference in the process or mode of the transmission and imprinting of the culture.

Two factors explain the present configuration of the world's large culture areas. First, emigration into empty or very thinly populated lands accounts for the Portuguese, Spanish, Anglo-Saxon, and Russian areas and played an important part in China during the first few centuries of the Christian era. Second, religion was the main operative force in the Indian and Arab areas and played an important part in Roman Europe and elsewhere.[27] A lower degree of racial prejudice and a greater willingness to intermarry also played a role in this process, especially in fairly densely settled regions, as distinct from the almost empty lands of Anglo North America and Southern Latin America.

Notes

I am indebted to Glen W. Bowersock, Peter Brown, Bernard Lewis, and Paula Sanders for their many helpful suggestions. I also benefited from searching criticism at the Davis Center Seminar at Princeton University, led by Lawrence Stone, and from the comments of two anonymous reviewers.

1. Figures on this subject are necessarily tentative. In 1985, China had 1.04 billion inhabitants, of whom 788 million used Mandarin and most of the rest Cantonese; Taiwan had another 20 million. India had 763 million, of whom 300 million spoke Hindi. The number of English speakers was given as 420 million, which obviously includes many people outside the Anglo-Saxon culture area; the United States had a population of 239 million, the United Kingdom 56 million, Canada 25 million (of whom 7 million were French-speaking), Australia 16 million, and New Zealand 3 million, or 340 million in all. The Soviet Union had 278 million inhabitants; in 1979, when the total was 264 million, 153 million reported that their mother tongue was Russian and another 61 million said that they spoke it fluently. The population of Latin America was 410 million. The number of French speakers was put at 114 million, but, as for English, this figure must include many from outside the cultural area; the population of France was 55 million, to which should be added another 5 million French-speaking Belgians and Swiss, that of Italy 57 million, of Spain 39 million, and of Portugal 10 million, or about 166 million in all. The number of Arabic speakers was given as 177 million; the population of the members of the Arab League, including Mauritania and Somalia, was 192 million, including non-Arabic speakers such as the Berbers of North Africa, the Kurds of Iraq, and the southern Sudanese. Population figures are from Central Intelligence Agency, *The World Factbook, 1985* (Washington, D.C., 1985); language figures from Mark S. Hoffman (ed.), *The World Almanac, 1987* (New York, 1987), 216, 559, 622.

2. For estimates of the population of the Roman, Arab, Byzantine, and Ottoman empires, see Issawi, "The Area and Population of the Arab Empire: An Essay in Speculation," in idem, *The Arab Legacy* (Princeton, 1981), 23–44; for the Seleucid Empire, Michael Grant, *From Alexander to Cleopatra* (New York, 1982), 48; for China, Hans Bielenstein, "The Census of China during the Period A.D. 2–742," *Bulletin of the Museum of Far Eastern Antiquities*, XIX (1947), 125–63; for Latin America and Indonesia, John D. Durand, "The Modern Expansion of World Population," *Proceedings of the American Philosophical Society*, 111 (1967), 137; for India, "Population," in Tapan Raychaudhuri and Irfan Habib (eds.), *The Cambridge Economic History of India* (Cambridge, 1982), 1, 163–66; 2, 466; for the Moghul Empire in 1600, a figure of 60–70 million has been suggested in Shireen Moosvi, "Production, Consumption and Population in Akbar's Time," *Indian Economic and Social History Review*, 10 (1973), 181–95; for the city of Venice, a figure

of 100,000 is given for both the end of the thirteenth century and 1500. See J. H. Clapham and Eileen Power (eds.), *The Cambridge Economic History of Europe* (Cambridge, 1942), 1, 326; Carlo Cipolla (ed.), *The Fontana Economic History of Europe: The Sixteenth and Seventeenth Centuries* (London, 1974), 22; for later figures, E. E. Rich and C. H. Wilson (eds.), *Cambridge Economic History of Europe* (Cambridge, 1967), 4, 35.

3. Assyria had its ups and downs. After a long period of independence, during which it expanded and contracted, it began a rapid period of conquest in 883 B.C. under Ashur-nasir-pal II, reaching the Mediterranean. A short decline (782–745) was followed by renewed conquests that included Babylonia, Egypt, and various Syrian states. The destruction of Assyria, by the Medo-Babylonian coalition, took place in 612–605 B.C.

4. Ibn Khaldun (trans. Charles Issawi), *An Arab Philosophy of History* (Princeton, 1987; reprint), 63–64. On the Arabs and Romans, see Issawi, "The Contribution of the Arabs to Islamic Civilization," in idem, *Arab Legacy*, 45–55; idem, "The Historical Role of Muhammad," ibid., 57–67.

5. See idem, "The Struggle for Linguistic Hegemony, 1780–1980," *American Scholar*, 50 (1981), 382–87.

6. It should be remembered that the Greeks founded many cities in Asia—over 20 by Alexander and about 70 by his Seleucid successors—though many of them soon wilted for lack of Greek immigrants.

7. Grant, *From Alexander*, 61, 69, 63. See also Francis E. Peters, *The Harvest of Hellenism* (New York, 1970); Arnaldo Momigliano, *Alien Wisdom: The Limits of Hellenism* (Cambridge, 1975); John Ferguson, *The Heritage of Hellenism* (New York, 1973).

8. George A. Buttrick (ed.), *The Interpreter's Dictionary of the Bible* (Nashville, Tenn., 1962), s. v. "Versions," 749–760 (I owe this reference to John Marks). See also Leighton D. Reynolds and N. G. Wilson, *Scribes and Scholars* (Oxford, 1974; 2nd ed.), 48. It has been claimed, among others by St. Jerome, that St. Matthew's Gospel was originally composed in Hebrew and then translated into Greek by an unknown hand; this claim is rejected by modern scholars. It is, however, accepted that there was an Aramaic or Syriac *Gospel of the Nazaraeans*, which had "a certain relationship" with that of St. Matthew. See John N. D. Kelly, *Jerome: His Life, Writings and Controversies* (New York, 1975), 65, and references therein.

9. The first recognition of French as a distinct language was in 813, when the Council of Tours decreed that certain homilies, delivered in Latin, be translated into Rustic Roman. In 842, Louis the German and Charles the Bold took their oaths at Strasbourg in both German and Rustic Roman. (See Mildred K. Pope, *From Latin to Modern French* [Manchester, 1934], 12–13; Peter Richard, *A History of the French Language* [London, 1974], 27–29.) Charles Thomas, *Christianity in Roman Britain* (Berkeley, 1981), 244.

10. Arnold H. M. Jones, *The Later Roman Empire* (Baltimore, 1986; orig. pub. 1964), 992. See also Raymond Van Dam, *Leadership and Community in Late Antique Gaul* (Berkeley, 1985), 15.

11. Thomas, *Christianity*, 64–65; John Morris, *The Age of Arthur* (New York, 1973), 407; Kenneth Jackson, *Language and History in Early Britain* (Edinburgh, 1953), 95–106, 116–21.

12. Ibid., 114. See also Robin G. Collingwood and John N. L. Myres, *Roman Britain and the English Settlements* (Oxford, 1937), 308–24; Jackson, 119; Cesare Foligno, "The Transmission of the Legacy," in Cyril Bailey (ed.), *The Legacy of Rome* (Oxford, 1923), 32.

13. Samuel Dill, *Roman Society in Gaul* (New York, 1966; orig. pub. 1926), 356–94; Albert Lecoy de la Marche, *La Fondation de la France* (Lille, 1893), 100; Dill, *Roman Society*, 502, 440.

14. Van Dam, *Leadership*, 133, 141–47. See also Dill, *Roman Society*, 487, 81.

15. Earl of Cromer [Evelyn Baring], *Ancient and Modern Imperialism* (New York, 1910).

16. Ibid., 93.

17. As quoted in Bernal Diaz (trans. J. M. Cohen), *The Conquest of New Spain* (Harmondsworth, 1963), 159 (I owe this reference to John Elliott).

18. Jean-Claude Vatin, *L'Algérie politique: histoire et société* (Paris, 1983), 26.

19. Virgil (trans. Edward Taylor), *Aeneid* (London, 1940), Bk. 6, st. 114 (orig. Bk. 6, 2, 852–53).

20. Cromer, *Ancient and Modern Imperialism*, 19–71.

21. See Marshall Hodgson, *The Venture of Islam* (Chicago, 1974), 2, 14–17, 257–59; Lawrence Browne, *The Eclipse of Christianity in Asia* (New York, 1966; orig. pub. 1933), 161–74.

22. For Ottoman administration, see Halil Inalcik, *The Ottoman Empire* (London, 1973), 89–118. For Iranian administration, see Ehsan Yarshater (ed.), *The Cambridge History of Iran* (Cambridge, 1983), 3, 723–38, 744–46, 760. A remarkable parallel between Persian and English may be noted. Following the Arab and Norman conquests, Arabic and Norman French, respectively, became the languages of the court, law, learning, and literature. However, after 300 years or so, a new language emerged, represented by such poets as Rudaqi (fl. 930s) and Firdawsi (d.c. 1020) and William Langland (c. 1330–1386) and Geoffrey Chaucer (c. 1343–1400), respectively. In both countries, the new language kept the old morphology and syntax (Middle Persian and Anglo-Saxon) but took about half of its vocabulary from the new (Arabic and Norman French), especially abstract terms. Arabic was the "Latin" as well as the Norman French of Iran, and therefore lasted much longer. Indeed, in the recent past Ayatollah Ruhollah Khomeini published several treatises in Arabic, and Arabic is still regarded as the preferable medium for Iranian clerics.

23. Ronald Syme, *Colonial Elites* (London, 1958), 17.

24. Glen W. Bowersock, *Roman Arabia* (Cambridge, Mass., 1983), 123–24.

25. This emigration does not seem to be closely correlated with the size of the population from which it issued. The Arab population was tiny (only

a small fraction of the Persian, for instance) and so was the Portuguese. The population of Spain, England, and even Russia until the eighteenth century, was small—considerably less than that of France, Italy, and Germany. Of the Romans, Indians, and Chinese, too little is known to warrant any statement.

26. Ibn Khaldun (ed. M. Quatremère), *Al-Muqaddima* (Paris, 1858), 1, 269.

27. Trade and trade diasporas have done much to diffuse religions, for example, Buddhism in Central and Southeast Asia, Hinduism in Southeast Asia, Christianity in Ethiopia and Southwest India, Islam in the Indian Ocean area and Africa, and so on. See Philip D. Curtin, *Cross-Cultural Trade in World History* (Cambridge, 1984). But, unless accompanied by large-scale migration, trade and trade diasporas are not sufficient to create a cultural area, as defined in this chapter.

THREE

SHELLEY AND THE NEAR EAST

Shelley was a marvellous lyric poet, but he was much more than that. A voracious and insatiable reader, he spent almost all his waking hours with books, even when eating or walking in city streets, and took in philosophy, science, history, and literature with equal zest. He was an extremely perceptive critic—one of the very first to recognize the genius of Keats, this "rival who will far surpass me," and he mourned him in one of his finest poems, "Adonaïs." He was equally appreciative of Byron and at once declared that *Don Juan* was his masterpiece—"every word is stamped with immortality." He was a good shot—as good as Byron. An excellent linguist, he translated Plato, Virgil, Spinoza, Dante, Tasso, Calderon, Goethe, and others (and also the *Marseillaise*). He studied the philosophers, including the English empiricists, the French materialists, and Kant, and had a special admiration for Plato and Bishop Berkeley.

He was also a keen and knowledgeable scientist, particularly interested in chemistry, electricity, astronomy, and meteorology (his early chemical and electrical experiments exposed him and those around to bodily harm and thoroughly messed up his rooms at home and at Oxford). Indeed, A. N. Whitehead goes so far as to say: "If Shelley had been born a hundred years later, the twentieth century would have seen a Newton among chemists." Less contestably, he points out: "It is unfortunate that Shelley's literary critics have, in this respect, so little of Shelley in their own mentality."[1]

Shelley looked to science for both illumination and practical application and saw clearly the use of chemistry for agriculture and the enormous potential of electric energy. Many passages in his poems—notably in "Prometheus," "Ode to the West Wind," and "The Cloud"—embody the science of their day, or even of a later day, and can be fully understood only in that light; this includes many verses which at first may strike the reader as incomprehensible, or indeed pure nonsense.[2]

Another aspect of Shelley's interest in science and technology showed in his financing, and active participation in, the construction of what would have been the first steamboat in the Mediterranean, intended to ply between Leghorn and Marseilles. The project cost him £400, but the world gained his delightful, humorous "Letter to Maria Gisborne," where he describes himself at work amid "great screws, and cones, and wheels, and grooved blocks."

But Shelley was too good a poet to believe that science alone could ensure salvation. In A Defence of Poetry (1821, published 1846) he puts it beautifully:

> The cultivation of those sciences which have enlarged the limits of the empire of man over the external world has for want of the poetical faculty proportionally circumscribed those of the internal world; and man, having enslaved the elements, remains himself a slave.

Shelley was a vegetarian and wrote a treatise on that subject. He was a strong feminist, as befitted the husband of Mary Wollstonecraft's daughter. The Revolt of Islam has that rousing line: "Can man be free if woman be a slave?" and his heroine is as strong and dedicated as his hero. He was also an amazingly kind, unselfish man, exceptionally and often foolishly generous with his time and money. Many stories told about him show an almost saintly quality. Byron, as shrewd and cynical an observer as one could wish for, described him as "without exception the best and least selfish man I ever knew." However, Shelley treated his first wife with a callousness that is hard to understand. It should also be added that he struck some people—including his father—as a lunatic.[3] But then

> The lunatic, the lover and the poet
> Are of imagination all compact.

And Shelley's white-hot imagination made him see and report many things that probably never happened.

Finally, and most important for our purpose, Shelley was passionately interested in politics from his earliest youth. A born rebel, he soon espoused every revolutionary cause, and came to be regarded as the most dangerous of the younger poets. Of course, he did his best to exasperate the Establishment with poems like *The Masque of Anarchy* and the sonnet "England in 1819." He positively courted unpopularity by his infantile habit of proclaiming his atheism on every possible occasion, even when he registered at a hotel.

Karl Marx, no mean authority, said that Shelley, had he lived, "would always have been one of the advanced-guard of socialism" and is reported to have stated that he "had inspired a good deal of . . . the Chartist movement." As late as the 1930s "a group of Communists in a Milwaukee jail were reported to have attempted to convert fellow prisoners by reading *Queen Mab* aloud"—and at about the same time hunger-marchers in Toronto chanted *The Masque of Anarchy*.

And yet, unnoticed by his enemies and also by many of his admirers, Shelley's view of revolution changed radically. Deeper study of the French Revolution convinced him that such uprisings merely replace one tyranny by another. The French, brutalized by king, Church, and nobles, behaved brutally when in power and called forth the Napoleonic reaction—which of course does not mean that oppression should be passively accepted. As Shelley wrote in his preface to *The Revolt of Islam* in 1817, when the panic created by the French Revolution was "gradually giving place to sanity":

> [I]t has ceased to be believed that whole generations of mankind ought to consign themselves to a hopeless inheritance of ignorance and misery, because a nation of men who had been dupes and slaves for centuries were incapable of conducting themselves with the wisdom and tranquillity of freemen as soon as some of their fetters were partially loosened.

Revolution demands a long and arduous moral preparation and should be carried out by passive resistance—calmly facing troops, not attacking them but never running away. This is very much what Gandhi practiced so successfully in India, though his inspiration came from other sources.

Shelley's political views are spelled out in *The Masque of Anarchy* and in his 1819 pamphlet, *A Philosophical View of Reform,* for which he could not find a publisher and which was not printed until 1920. It is a calm, closely reasoned call for constitutional, economic, and judicial reforms, almost all of which were implemented in the course of the next hundred years. It contains a quick view of history as the unfolding of liberty, in which his main landmarks are the birth of liberty in Greece, its suppression by Imperial Rome and the Catholic Church, and its gradual recovery during the Reformation, the establishment of the Dutch Republic, the English Revolutions, the American Revolution, and the French Revolution. He sees everywhere signs of the awakening of peoples—Germany, Spain, Latin America, and elsewhere. This brings him to the Near East.

In 1815, Shelley had read Simon Ockley's *History of the Saracens* (3 vols., 1708–1757), and before and after that he read and reread Gibbon. In 1820, he started to study Arabic. On 29 October he wrote to John Gisborne: "Can you tell me anything about Arabic grammars, dictionaries, and manuscripts, and whether they are vendible at Leghorn, and whether there are any native Arabs capable of teaching the language." And on 15 November to Thomas Love Peacock: "A school fellow of mine from India is staying with me and we are beginning Arabic together."[4] It is not clear how much progress he made, but in 1821 he wrote "From the Arabic: An Imitation." What the original could have been—or whether indeed there was a specific original—is not known. Most of his information on the Near East, however, must have come from what in the preface to *Hellas* he disparagingly called his "newspaper erudition."

In Shelley's vision, the fermentation of liberty was extending to Asia. He starts with India, whose development was to have such a great influence on the Near East, through its British rulers. Remarkably, Shelley regards Christianity—to which he was so opposed at home—as the first force of regeneration in India: "[I]t cannot be doubted but the zeal of the missionaries of what is called the Christian faith will produce beneficial innovation there, even by the application of dogmas and forms of what is here an outworn incumbrance." In addition, there are secular forces at work:

> Many native Indians have acquired, it is said, a competent knowledge in the arts and philosophy of Europe, and Locke and Hume and Rousseau are familiarly talked of in Brahminical society. But the thing to be sought is that they should as they would if they were free attain to a system of arts and literature of their own.

The works of Rammohan Roy (1772–1833) show that he was not exaggerating the degree of ferment.

Shelley begins his survey of the Near East with Iran. "Of Persia we know little but that it has been the theatre of sanguinary contests for power, and that it is now at peace. The Persians appear to be from organisation a beautiful, refined, and impassioned people and would probably soon be infected by the contagion of good."

What of the Jews? Here Shelley indulges in a bold speculation: "The Jews, that wonderful people which has preserved so long the symbols of their union, may reassume their ancestral seats." (It may be noted that, 30 years earlier, in "A Song of Liberty," William Blake had exclaimed, "O Jew, leave counting gold; return to thy oil and wine.")

Arabia? "In Syria and Arabia the spirit of human intellect has roused a sect of people called Wahabees, who maintain the Unity of God, and the equality of man, and their enthusiasm must go on 'conquering and to conquer' even if it must be repressed in its present shape."

Egypt? Shelley was appreciative of the work being done by Muhammad Ali (to whom, for some mysterious reason, he refers as Ottoman Bey):

> a person of enlightened views who is introducing European literature and arts, and is thus beginning that change which Time, the great innovator, will accomplish in that degraded country; and by the same means its sublime enduring monuments may excite lofty emotions in the hearts of the posterity of those who now contemplate them without admiration.

Here again he was right about the complete neglect and subsequent enthusiastic discovery by the Egyptians of their monuments. He adds an appreciative footnote:

> This person sent his nephew to Lucca to study European learnings, and when his nephew asked with reference to some branch of study at enmity with Mahometanism whether he was permitted to engage in it, he replied, "You are at liberty to do anything which will not injure another."

When it comes to Turkey, Shelley's attitude is very different. The Turks he saw only as the oppressors of the Greeks, the people who had devastated their lands. In this he was one of the first of many European liberals who execrated the Turks as enemies of freedom and national independence in the Balkans and Near East. Hegel, refuting Geographical Determinism with his devastating "Where the Greeks once loved the Turks now live," is another contemporary example. It is perhaps worth pointing out that in *Frankenstein* Mary Shelley has a villainous Turk and his admirable daughter—born of a Christian Arab mother and herself referred to as such.

Shelley's love and admiration for the Ancient Greeks was one of his strongest passions. Again and again he repeats that almost all that was worthwhile in Europe came from Greece. Hence his statement in this pamphlet:

> The Turkish Empire is in its last stage of ruin, and it cannot be doubted but that the time is approaching when the deserts of Asia Minor and of Greece will be colonized by the overflowing population of countries less enslaved and debased, and that the climate and the scenery which was the birthplace of all that is wise and beautiful will not remain forever the spoil of wild beasts and unlettered Tartars

—a prophecy that was only half correct.

One might have expected *The Revolt of Islam*, written in 1817, to deal with the Near East; but although it is located in Greece and the overthrown tyrant is named Othman, there is no suggestion of any local color or background. The title was apparently suggested by Shelley's friends in England, to remove suspicions that he was attacking Christianity. However the outbreak of the Greek War of Independence in 1821 immediately focused his attention on that country.

Like many passionate Hellenists, Shelley took a dim view of modern Greeks—just as many Orientalists think very poorly of Arabs or Persians. Byron had contributed to this with his notes to Canto Two of *Childe Harold*, and Shelley's friend Trelawney had taken him onto a Greek trading ship whose dirt and squalor reminded him more of Hell than Hellas. Another Greek captain he knew was opposed to the war because it was bad for trade. And, whether Shelley was aware of it or not, the fact is that the Greek Phanariots—the rich merchants and bankers of Constantinople—and the Patriarch were also opposed to the revolt.

But to Shelley none of that really mattered. As he put it in the Preface to *Hellas*:

> If in many instances [the Greek] is degraded by moral and political slavery to the practice of the basest vices it engenders—and that below the level of ordinary degradation—let us reflect that the corrup-

tion of the best produces the worst, and that habits which subsist only in relation to a peculiar state of social institution may be expected to ease as soon as that relation is dissolved.

Besides, progress was already taking place. Greeks were returning home from "the universities of Italy, Germany and France. . . . The University of Chios contained before the breaking out of the revolution eight hundred students, and among them several Germans and Americans." Above all Shelley was inspired by Prince Alexander Mavrocordato, one of the leaders of the revolt, whom he got to know well at Leghorn. In the Preface to *Hellas* he repeats: "We are all Greeks. Our laws, our literature, our religion, our arts have their root in Greece." But for Greece, Rome would have "spread no illumination with her arms."

In another striking prophecy, Shelley couples Rome with the United States:

Rome was, and young Atlantis shall become
The wonder, or the terror, or the tomb
Of all whose step wakes Power lulled in
her davage lair.

But Greece is different:

             . . . a hermit-child
Whose fairest thoughts and limbs were built
To woman's growth, by dreams so mild,
She knew not pain or guilt.

The whole civilized world should have rushed to aid Greece. Instead,

The English permit their own oppressors to act according to their natural sympathy with the Turkish tyrant, and to brand upon their name the indelible blot of an alliance with the enemies of domestic happiness, of Christianity and civilisation.

Russia desires to possess, not to liberate, Greece; and is contented to see the Turks, its natural enemies, and the Greeks, its intended slaves, enfeeble each other until one or both fall into its net. The wise and generous policy of England would have consisted in establishing the independence of Greece, and in maintaining it both against Russia and the Turk—but when was the oppressor generous and just.

He could not forsee the tangled strains of events that led to the short lived Anglo-Franco-Russian agreement and the Battle of Navarino.

The drama is modeled on Aeschylus' *Persae*, but whereas the latter could conclude with a resounding Greek victory over the Persians, Shelley seems to imply that the Turks would crush the Greek revolt. Unlike so many of his earlier works, this one contains no propagandistic caricatures or oversimplification. Sultan Mahmud is no mere bloodthirsty tyrant but a true tragic figure. Shelley does however slip up on his Arabic—perhaps because of the exigencies of the pentameter:

> *The mingled battle-cry—ha! hear I not*
> *"En toutoi nike" "Allah-illa-Allah"?*

He put another premature prediction in the mouth of the ghost of Mehmet the Conqueror: "Islam must fall."

The Greek revolt will be crushed but the peoples of Europe—of France, of Germany, of Spain—will liberate themselves and then Greece. And in his beautiful choruses Shelley soars above the present to an idealized, Platonic world.

> *The world's great age begins anew*
> *The golden years return . . .*

> *And Greece, which was dead, is arisen!*

But the chorus ends on a tired, despairing note:

> *The world is weary of its past*
> *Oh might it die or rest at last.*

And that, perhaps, is how every study of the Near East, with its blood-soaked historical burdens, should end.

Notes

1. A. N. Whitehead, *Science and the Modern World* (1926), p. 104.

2. For an excellent study of this aspect, see Desmond King-Hele, *Shelley, His Thought and Work* (1960), ch. 8. I am indebted to this book for various references throughout this chapter: see, in particular, pp. 296, 322, 365, 45, 149.

3. See Newman Ivey White, *Shelley* (1940), Vol. 2, pp. 382, 419, and, for later references, pp. 417, 541–44, 329.

4. Percy Bysshe Shelley, *Complete Works* (Julian edition, London, 1926–1929), Vol. 10, pp. 216, 223.

FOUR

IBN KHALDUN ON ANCIENT HISTORY

A Study in Sources

What did Ibn Khaldun (1332–1406) know about the history of classical and preclassical civilizations, especially about Greek and Roman history? Judging from the *Muqaddimah*, very little, but considerably more if one takes the *'Ibar* into account. The discrepancy between the two books is worth examining, as well as Ibn Khaldun's sources.

AL-MUQADDIMAH

Like other Arab historians, Ibn Khaldun had only a summary, but essentially correct, knowledge of the history of pre-Islamic peoples. Of course, Jews and early Christians were regarded as being in a special position, having successively been the repositories of divine revelation until the advent of Islam, and more was known about them. He was aware that mighty, ancient civilizations had flourished:

> The old Persian nations, the Syrians, the Nabataeans, the Tubba's [Yemenis], the Israelites and the Copts [Egyptians], all once existed. They had their own particular institutions in respect of dynastic and territorial arrangements, their own politics, crafts, languages, technical terminologies, as well as their own ways of dealing with their fellow men and handling their cultural institutions. Their [historical] relics testify to that. They were succeeded by the later Persians, the Byzantines [Rum] and the Arabs. . . . [T]hen the days of Arab rule

were over. . . . [T]he power was seized by others, by non-Arabs like
the Turks in the east, the Berbers in the west, and the European
Christians [Franks].[1]

But, as he went on to say, very little knowledge was transmitted
about these civilizations: "The sciences of only one nation, the
Greeks, have come down to us, because they were translated through
al-Ma'mun's efforts. . . . [O]f the sciences of others, nothing has
come to our attention."[2]

Moreover, Ibn Khaldun had a quite accurate notion of the chronology of those peoples. The Jews' "rule in Syria [Sham] lasted about
1,400 years"—presumably from Moses to Herod. In Syria, the "Roman dynasties succeeded them [the Greeks] for six hundred years,"
presumably from Augustus to the Arab conquest. As for the Copts,
"their political power lasted three thousand years," presumably from
the First Dynasty of the Ancient Egyptians to the Macedonian
conquest. "They were succeeded there by the Greeks and the Romans, and then by Islam, which abrogated everything." In Yemen,
the "Arabs ruled continuously, ever since the time of the Amale-
kites and the Tubba's." As for Iraq, it was for thousands of years
"ruled continuously by the Nabateans and the Persians, that is the
Chaldeans, the Kayyanids [the Achaemenids], the Sassanians [al-
Kisrawiyah], and after them, the Arabs."[3] Given all this, the paucity
of historial information in the Muqaddimah on Greece and Rome
stands out starkly.

Because of the translation of numerous Greek scientific and
philosophical texts, and their intensive study by Muslim thinkers,
Ibn Khaldun was quite familiar with Greek intellectual and scientific
history. He mentioned the names and works of Euclid, Apollonius,
Theodosius, and Menelaus in mathematics; Ptolemy in astonomy;
and Galen in medicine. He also noted the Greek contribution to op-
tics and physics. On logic and metaphysics he had much to say, most
of it on Aristotle.[4] Like other Muslim scholars, he was not interested
in Greek literature or art, though he noted that "there were poets
among the Persians and among the Greeks." The Greek poet Homer
was mentioned and praised by Aristotle in the Logic.[5] He also noted
that the Greeks had temples and that, like the Persians before them,
they dug out treasure from Egyptian graves.[6] The following statement is also worth noting: "The intellectual sciences are said to have
come to the Greeks from the Persians, [at the time] when Alexander
killed Darius and gained control of the Achaemenid empire. At that

time he appropriated the books and sciences of the Persians."[7] This may possibly be an echo of the earlier Oriental contribution to Ionian science and philosophy.

Ibn Khaldun, however, was completely uninterested in the political history of Greece. The only person mentioned is Alexander, who studied under Artistotle, overthrew the Persian Empire, built Alexandria, and was credited with fabulous adventures, including the building of a great wall in Central Asia to keep out Gog and Magog.[8]

Ibn Khaldun knew much less about Rome and had a curiously distorted view of its empire. But he had two important insights. First, that the Greeks and Romans had closer affinities than those existing between other peoples; in his own words, "Their [the Greeks'] rule was wiped out and transferred to their brethren, the Rum [Romans]."[9] Second, that the Romans fell well below the Greeks in scientific achievement but preserved the latter's writings:

> When the Greek dynasty [Macedonians] was destroyed and the Roman emperors seized power and adopted Christianity, the intellectual sciences were shunned by them, as religious groups and their laws require. [But] they continued to have a permanent life in scientific writing and treatments which were preserved in their libraries.
>
> The [Roman Emperors] later on took possession of Syria. The [ancient] scientific books continued to exist during their [rule].[10]

Ibn Khaldun was fully aware that Rome took over Greek rule in Egypt, Syria, and other parts of the Eastern Mediterranean and survived as Byzantium. Like other Arab writers—and like the Byzantines themselves—he used the same name, "Rum," for both Romans and Byzantines. He was also aware that the Romans spoke Latin, which was distinct from Greek: "then [third] there is Latin, the language of the Byzantines [Romans]. When they adopted Christianity . . . they translated the Torah and the books of the Israelite prophets into their language, in order to be able to derive the law from [scripture] as easily as possible. Thus, they came to be more interested in their own language and writing than [in] any other."[11] "Matthew wrote his Gospel in Jerusalem in Hebrew. It was translated into Latin by John, the son of Zebedee, one of [the Apostles]. [The Apostle] Luke wrote his Gospel in Latin for a Roman dignitary. [The Apostle] John, son of Zebedee, wrote his Gospel in Rome. Peter wrote his Gospel in Latin and ascribed it to his pupil Mark."[12] He was also aware that Latin was still used in Spain.[13]

In these circumstances, it is surprising to discover that Ibn Khaldun does not seem to have known that Rome dominated the Western Mediterranean and, for many centuries, ruled the two regions with which he was most familiar, Spain and North Africa, or that it built the great monuments he saw there.

For Spain, Ibn Khaldun was explicit. The Goths had ruled the country for thousands of years before the Arab conquest (in reality only for about 250 years) and were a highly civilized people. No mention is made of Rome. Explaining why Spain was highly urbanized, he stated: "The customs of sedentary culture also became firmly rooted in Spain, later succeeded by the Umayyad realm. Both dynasties were great, therefore, the customs of sedentary culture continued and became firmly established in Spain."[14] This is echoed some pages later: "Sedentary culture had become deeply rooted in Spain through the stability given it by the Umayyad dynasty, the preceding dynasty and the *reyes de taifas*, successors to [the Umayyads] and so on. Therefore, sedentary culture had reached in [Spain] a stage that had not been reached in any other region except, reportedly, in the 'Iraq, Syria and Egypt."[15]

Regarding North Africa, Ibn Khaldun was more ambiguous. His general picture is given in the following passage, explaining why, in contrast to Spain, Egypt, and Syria, North Africa was not urbanized: "The reason for this is that these regions belonged to the Berbers for thousands of years before Islam. All their civilization was a Bedouin [i.e., nomadic] civilization. . . . [T]he dynasties of European Christians [Franks] and Arabs who ruled [the Berbers] did not rule long enough for their sedentary culture to take firm root [among them]."[16] In other passages, he mentions the Berbers and Vandals as the sole inhabitants of North Africa.[17] But in a very interesting chapter on fleets, in which he shows a firm grasp of the relation between sea power and the Crusades, he says:

> The Byzantines [Rum], the European Christians [Franks] and the Goths lived on the northern shore of the Mediterranean. Most of their wars and most of their commerce was by sea. They were skilled in navigating [the Mediterranean] and in naval war. When these people coveted the possession of the southern shore, as the Byzantines [coveted] Ifriqiyah and the Goths [coveted] the Maghrib, they crossed over in their fleets and took possession of it. Thus they achieved superiority over the Berbers and deprived them of their power. They had populous cities there, such as Carthage, Sbeitla, Jalula, Murnaq, Cherchel and Tangier. The ancient master of Carthage used to fight

the master of Rome [an acho of the Punic Wars? Or of the Vandal raids?] and to send fleets against him.[18]

It is noteworthy that, although Ibn Khaldun was fully aware of the Roman monuments in Spain and North Africa, he nowhere attributes them to Rome. Among those he mentions are the "bridge over the river at Cordoba, and, as well, the arches of the aqueduct over which water is brought into Carthage, the monuments of Cherchel in the Maghrib."[19] At one point, he describes the arches of the aqueduct at Carthage as "'Adi."[20] Again he states, "The inhabitants of the cities in Ifriqiyah believe that the European Christians [Franks] who lived in Ifriqiyah before Islam, buried their property and entrusted its [hiding place] to written lists, until such time as they might find a way to dig it up again."[21] And, "formerly, the whole region between the Sudan [sub-Saharan Africa] and the Mediterranean had been settled. This [fact] is attested by the relics of civilization there, such as monuments, architectural sculpture, and the visible remains of villages and hamlets."[22] But, although Ibn Khaldun was fully aware that these monuments were pre-Islamic, no hint is given of their Roman origin. Clearly, Ibn Khaldun failed to take in the magnitude of the cultural effects of the 600-year-old rule of Rome in North Africa.

Where, however, Rome impinged on the Jews and early Christians (i.e., on the proto-Muslims), he was more aware of its history. Ibn Khaldun was well informed on Jewish history and had a clear understanding of its periodization. Israelite "rule in Syria lasted about 1,400 years."[23] For about 400 years the Israelites did not have a king: "[T]heir only concern was to establish their religion, the person from among them who was in charge of their religion was called the Kohen." Then comes an account of their wars with the inhabitants of Syria and of their kings, Saul, David, and Solomon, and the split among the latter's successors into two dynasties. There follows a short description of the deportation of the Jews by Nebuchadnezzar, of their return under an Achaemenid king, of the Macedonian conquest, and of their revolt under the Hasmoneans:

> Eventually their power was destroyed. [The Romans] advanced toward Jerusalem, the seat of the children of Herod, relatives by marriage of the Hasmoneans and the last remnant of the Hasmonean dynasty. They laid Jerusalem in ruins and exiled [the Jews] to Rome and the regions beyond. This was the second destruction of the temple. The Jews call it "the Great Exile." After that they had no royal authority, because they had lost their group feeling. They remained afterwards under the domination of the Romans and their successors.

He also gives a slightly garbled list of the books of the Old Testament.[24] Elsewhere, he gives further details of Jewish history and mentions Titus, the conqueror of Jerusalem.

Ibn Khaldun was also well informed on the early history of Christianity, giving the names of the Apostles and Evangelists, a somewhat garbled version of the New Testament, and a brief account of the various sects.[25] As for the Roman connection: "Then, the religion of the Messiah was adopted by the Romans. It became their religious practice to venerate the Messiah [Jesus]. The Roman rulers vacillated, adopting Christianity at one time and giving it up at another, until Constantine appeared. His mother Helena became a Christian." There follows an account of her journey to Jerusalem and her building of the Holy Sepulchre.[26] He also mentions Nero, "the fifth Roman emperor," who killed the Apostle Peter.[27]

AL-ʿIBAR

As its title indicated, Ibn Khaldun's *Kitab al-ʿIbar* is concerned with the history of the Arabs and Berbers, but, like any self-respecting medieval historian, Ibn Khaldun begins his story with Creation. He devotes 236 pages, out of a total of some 3,700 pages, to pre-Arab history. Of these, 12 pages are concerned with Greek history and 36 with Roman history, in addition to 31 on the Persians and 29 on the Jews.[28] Throughout, Ibn Khaldun follows three chronologies: the Hebrew one of the creation of the world, the Greek one following Alexander's death, and the Roman AUC (*ab urbe condita*) from the foundation of Rome.[29]

The section on Greece[30] adds somewhat to the account in *al-Muqaddimah*. Both the Greeks (*al-Ighriq*) and the Romans (*al-Latiniyyun*) are described as descendants of Yavan, the son of Japhet (see Genesis, chapter 10) and, together with the Goths, as inhabitants of the area lying between the Mediterranean and the enveloping ocean. Among the Greek peoples were the Lacedaemonians, the Athenians, the Achaians, and the Arcadians. These peoples fought each other and the Latins and were subdued by the Persian Achaemenids and forced to pay tribute in the form of egg-like gold nuggets. Nothing more is said about the classical period, and there is no hint of the political structure or development of the city states.

The Hellenistic period receives more attention. Philip, son of Matryush (Amyntas) and a Persian lady, obtained the crown of Macedon around the year 353 B.C. He destroyed a Greek city (Thebes?) and built the city of Macedon; he was a lover of wisdom and therefore attracted many learned men to his court, including Aristotle. He subjugated the Greeks and ruled over the area between Alamaniya (Germany) and Armenia. He wanted to build Constantinope (sic) but was prevented by the Germans (a reference to his unsuccessful siege of Byzantium?).

There follows a fairly accurate account of Alexander's conquests (which included China!), of his foundation of two Alexandrias—in Sind and Egypt—and of his death in Babylon at the age of 42 (33) after a 12-(14-)year reign, possibly by poisoning. This section contains an account of Greek philosophy, from Thales to Plato, Aristotle, and Galen.

In a somewhat confused account, Ibn Khaldun describes the division of the empire under Alexander's successors: Ptolemy in Egypt, Philip in Macedonia, Demetrius in Syria, and Seleucus in Persia and the East. These men fought each other, but Ptolemy was the victor, conquering Palestine and deporting the Jewish leaders to Egypt; his family ruled Egypt for 300 years. His successor, Philadelphus, freed the Jewish captives, restored the plundered vessels to the Temple, and gathered 70 Jewish priests, who translated the Torah into Greek and Latin. There follows an account of the various Ptolemies, ending with Cleopatra. She invaded the Roman lands and penetrated Spain through the Pyrenees, married Antony, was defeated by Augustus, and killed herself with a poisonous snake. Her story obviously fascinated Arab historians, and on that topic Ibn Khaldun quotes al-Bayhaqi, al-Mas'udi, and Ibn al-'Amid (where Christian sources are mentioned) as well as Orosius. Of the other rulers, only Antiochus is mentioned; a fairly detailed account is given in that context of the Maccabean revolt. A more detailed account is given in the section on Jewish history, which brings the story down to the destruction of the Temple.[31]

Ibn Khaldun's account of Roman history was more detailed and accurate because his sources were more abundant. An introductory chapter[32] tells of the Trojan origin of Rome and tries to fit its legendary chronology into that of the Jews. Romulus and Amash (Remus) founded the city of Rome—which was 20 miles long and 12 miles wide, with walls rising 48 dira' (ells) high, and among the greatest cities in the world. After Romulus came five kings, the last of whom violated a married woman (Lucretia), who killed herself. The Romans then resolved not to have a monarchy but to be governed by 320 senators (*shuyukh*) or by a council of 70 ministers (*wazir*) called consuls (*qunshulush*). According to Ben Gorion, the foundation of Rome was contemporaneous with the reign of David (1000–961 B.C.), but Orosius says it was in the time of Hezekiah (715–687 B.C.). This system continued for 700 years, during which the Romans fought their neighbors and the Greeks, then the Persians, and ruled Syria, Egypt, and Spain, then Sicily and North Africa. Then came Julius Caesar, son of Gaius, who was the first of the Caesars.

The next chapter[33] deals with the relations of the Romans (*al-Kaytam*—*Kittim*, Genesis 10:4) and Africa (i.e., Tunisia). Carthage was built by Didan [Dido], "son" (*sic*), of Elisha, who was descended from Esau, 72 years before Rome. Led by a ruler named Malkun, the Carthaginians conquered Sicily and waged war against the Romans and Alexander's people (Greeks) over Sardinia; that was in the fiftieth year after the foundation of Rome. Peace was then concluded and Amilga (Hamilcar) sent his son Anibil (Hannibal)[34] to the land of the Franks, which he conquered. Rome dispatched its generals against him, but he defeated them repeatedly and sent his brother Ashdrubal (Hasdrubal) to rule Spain. The Romans, however, captured about 40 Sicilian cities and followed Anibil to Africa, defeated him, then besieged him in Carthage. Other Roman generals defeated and killed Ashdrubal in Spain. Peace was concluded on payment by Carthage of 3,000 *qintar* of silver. However, Anibil supported the kings of Syria (Seleucids) in their wars against Rome and died by poisoning. The Romans then conquered Spain, crossed over to Africa, and destroyed it in its nine-hundredth year, the seven-hundredth of Rome's foundation. War then broke out between Rome and the King of Nubia (Numidia?), who was supported by the Berbers but was defeated and died in captivity—and that was during the reign of Ptolemy. The Romans rebuilt Carthage, 22 years after its destruction, and it prospered.

The following chapter[35] relates the history of the Caesars. According to Orosius, the Romans were at first subject to the Greeks, but, after the death of Alexander and the ensuing wars, the Romans repeatedly attacked Africa, destroying Carthage, and conquered Spain, Syria, and Hijaz. For 700 years, they chose their ministers by lot until Julius, son of Gaius, Caesar, who had been ripped out of his mother's womb after her death, set out to conquer the lands of the Franks and Galicians, Britain and Lisbon. The ministers, fearing that he would establish absolute rule over them, killed him after five years' rule. However, his nephew, Octavian, avenged him and took his place, ruling over the northern part of the world for 56 years, in the forty-second of which Christ was born. Ibn al-'Amīd's slightly different and more detailed version is then given. It brings in the story of Cleopatra and Antony, the life of Jesus and the Apostles, and the spread of Christianity and the persecutions it endured from the Jews and Romans. Augustus' successors were Tiberius, Gaius, Claudius, and Nero, the sixth of the Caesars. The length of their reigns is given, but the relationship between them is, not surprisingly, confused.

There follows an account of the struggle for succession after the death of Nero, and garbled versions are given of the names of Galba, Otho, and Vitellius. Bishbishan (Vespasian) seized power and was succeeded by his son Titus, who fought the Jews and destroyed Jerusalem with great slaughter and who was learned and virtuous. Titus' brother (Dumurian, according to Orosius; Damistianus, according to Ibn al-'Amīd) succeeded him; he was tyrannical and persecuted both Christians and Jews. Then came the son of Titus (*sic*), Berma (Nerva), who was a good ruler and adopted Trajan, a native of Malaga and one of his great generals, who ruled for 17 (19) years. His successor was Andrianus (Hadrian), who ruled for 21 years, persecuted the Christians, destroyed Jerusalem, and dug a freshwater canal (actually, it was Trajan who had the canal built) between the Nile and the Gulf of Suez, which later silted. Many learned men flourished under him. He was succeeded by his son Antonish (Antoninus), who was called "the merciful Caesar" and reigned for 21 or 22 years (23). His successor was his brother Auralish, or the younger Antonius (Marcu Aurelius), who fought the Persians led by Ardashir; in his reign, there was a great plague and a drought. The period of confusion that followed the death of Commodus is reflected in the various names mentioned by Ibn Khaldun, who quotes inconsistent sources; among the emperors mentioned are Severus, Alexander, Maximinus, Aurelian, and Gallienus. The chapter ends with an account of Diocletian, who reigned 20 or 21 years, his persecution of the Christians, the division of the empire between Galerius and Constantius, and the accession of Constantine, son of the Christian Helena. Throughout, Ibn Khaldun devotes much space to Christian ecclesiastical history, giving the names of patriarchs, discusses the wars with the Persians, and mentions the Gothic invasion of the Balkans.

The last three chapters of the pre-Arab section may be dealt with summarily, since, strictly speaking, they fall mostly outside the scope of this chapter. The first[36] is entitled "An account of the victorious Latin Caesars, the *Kaytam,* and the strengthening of their kingdom in Constantinople, then in Syria until the Muslim conquest and thereafter until the extinction of their rule."

This chapter opens with a sentence that has a Gibbonian ring: "These victorious Caesars were among the greatest and most celebrated kings of the world. They ruled the lands bordering the Mediterranean from Spain through Rome, Constantinople, Syria, Egypt, Alexandria and Africa to Morocco. They fought the Turks and Persians in the East and the blacks [*al-Sudan*] in the West, in Nubia and beyond." Originally pagans (*majus*), they adopted Christianity under Constantine, the thirty-third of the Caesars, who defeated and killed Maksimanus (Maxentius) at the (Milvian) bridge and established his rule in Byzantium. Much of the chapter is devoted to ecclesiastical history, noting the controversy between Arius and Athanasius, Julian's apostasy, the various church councils, the vicissitudes of the churches of Egypt and Syria, and the split between Melkites and Jacobites. Here Ibn Khaldun's sources were more abundant, and he quotes many historians, Muslim and other, often noting the inconsistencies in their narratives. An account is also given of the wars of the Romans with the Persians and the Goths; some of the latter were Arians, and he mentions how they sacked Rome. Among the emperors mentioned are Valentinian, Valens, Theodosius, Arcadius, Honorius, Marcian, Leo, Zeno—who ordered all women writers (*katibah*) to be killed (an echo of Hypatia's death?)— Anastasius, Tiberius, Justin, Justinian, and Maurice. Heraclius's wars with the Persians are given in much detail.

The next chapter[37] is entitled "An account of the Caesar kings from Heraclius and the [establishment of the] Muslim state to the extinction of their power and the disappearance of their condition." It gives a detailed account of the Arab conquest of Syria and Egypt, the sieges of Constantinople, and the subsequent expeditions in Anatolia under the Umayyads, Abbasids, and Hamdanids. Various rulers are mentioned, including Constantine, Nicephorus, Basil the Slav, Leo, Romanus, Michael, and Theodora. In addition, mention is made of the relations of the Byzantines with the Bulgars, Armenians, Russians, Turks, and Seljuks. A detailed account is given of the sack of Constantinople by the Franks (Crusaders) and mention is made of the part played by both the French (Fransis) and the blind doge of Venice (Dandolo). The recapture of

Constantinople by Lascaris, the Tatar (Mongol) invasion, and the predominace of the Ottomans conclude the chapter. Throughout, Ibn Khaldun's main sources are Muslim, including al-Mas'udi and Ibn al-Athir.

The last chapter[38] is concerned with the Goths, especially in Spain until the Arab conquest. Originally known as al-Sisiyyun (Scythians?), with a kinship with the Chinese, they inhabited the lands between the Persians and Greeks, fought the Romans, and, led by Antarik (Alaric), sacked Rome. They then moved west, to Spain, which was inhabited by the Iberians and where Roman rule had weakened, followed by three tribes, one of which, the Fandalus (Vandals), gave its name to Andalusia. An account is given of their wars with the Franks and the Arab invasion, and mention is made of their kings.

It should be added that the Romans make one more appearance—that is, apart from the brief accounts of the Arab conquest of Syria and Egypt.[39] In the books dealing with Berbers (vols. 6 and 7 in the Beirut edition), Ibn Khaldun has passages describing North Africa before the Arab conquest.[40] As mentioned earlier, the Romans conquered the country and destroyed Carthage. They built several cities that later became famous—Sbeitla, Jalula, Murnaq, and others—whose remains testify to their size and solid construction and which the Arabs destroyed during their conquest. The Berbers became Christians under Roman rule, though some professed Judaism. But outside the garrisoned cities, they lived with impunity from the Romans and Franks under their kings and chieftains, though they paid a tribute to Heraclius, king of Constantinople, as did the rulers of Alexandria, Egypt, and Cyrenaica. When the Arabs invaded North Africa, authority was, in fact, in the hands of the Franks. Their king, Juraijir or Jurjir (Gregory), raised an army of 120,000 Franks, Romans, and Berbers, but he was defeated and killed, the remnants of the army fleeing to various strong places. The Arabs stayed in the plains and from there fought their enemies.

Clearly, there is a great discrepancy between the knowledge of Roman history shown in *al-Muqaddimah* and that in *al-'Ibar*. A possible explanation is that, in the former, Ibn Khaldun was not interested in the details of history; certainly not in those of pre-Islamic history. But this would not explain some of his inaccurate statements, such as that Spain had been ruled by the Goths for thousands of years, and his surprisingly limited knowledge of Roman history. In *al-'Ibar*, the references are more detailed.

A more plausible hypothesis is the following: Ibn Khaldun wrote *al-Muqaddimah* in the space of three years, in Qal'at Ibn Salamah, a fortress in the mountains of Oran, where he was given refuge. He was an exile, disillusioned with politics. He had left his library in Tunis and had very few books at his disposal. This was most fortunate, since it compelled him to concentrate his thought and work out his ideas, unencumbered by scholarly impedimenta. It is noteworthy that in the *al-Muqaddimah* there are no references to Ibn al-'Amīd or Orosius and only one to Ben Gorion (Josippon),[41] who were later to constitute his main sources on classical history. *Al-'Ibar*, however, was written in Tunis, where he had access to large libraries and government records (*dawawin*),[42] on which he drew fully. But he did not bother to revise *al-Muqaddimah* in the light of what he had learned later, except in some minor respects.

SOURCES

Orosius

The non-Muslim source on which Ibn Khaldun relied most heavily, which he quotes most often, in *al-'Ibar*—but does not mention in *al-Muqaddimah*—was Paulus Orosius's (Hurosiush), *Historiarum Adversus Paganos Libri Septem*. Orosius (circa 385–420) as a younger friend of Saint Augustine, at whose urging he wrote this apology for Christianity. It is a survey of world history, from Adam to his own times, designed to prove that Christianity was not responsible for contemporary woes by showing that previous ages had experienced even greater sufferings and that Christian morals had, on the contrary, somewhat alleviated them.[43] The book enjoyed great popularity in late classical and medieval times, and a free translation into Anglo-Saxon was made by King Alfred the Great.

Around 950 A.D., an Arabic translation was made, from a Latin manuscript sent by the Byzantine emperor Constantine Porphyrogenitus to the Umayyad caliph Al-Hakam, by a Christian and a Muslim scholar both living in Cordoba.[44] As far as we know, Orosius's *History* is the only book written in Latin to have been translated into Arabic,[45] and Ibn Khaldun is the only Arab scholar to have made significant use of it.[46] In other words, the chapters in *al-'Ibar* based on Orosius are the only noteworthy irruption of Latinity in Arabic literature.

Orosius drew on many sources: Livy, Eutropius, Florus, Caesar,

Suetonius, Tacitus, Justin, Sallust, and others as well as on such Christian authors as Eusebius-Jerome, Augustine, and, of course, the Bible. He also occasionally quotes such classics as Virgil.[47] But the purpose of his writing strictly limited the scope and interest of his work. He was not concerned with constitutional and political developments, still less with social or economic questions, but almost solely with wars, natural catastrophes, massacres, treacheries, and other products of sin and causes of misery. This meant that Ibn Khaldun's knowledge of Roman and other classical history was similarly limited, and the use he could make of such history was strictly constrained.

Naturally, Orosius had his share of errors and inconsistencies. In addition, it is likely that the translators worked on a corrupt manuscript and introduced further errors of their own. Moreover, there are certain passages in the Arabic text that are taken not from Orosius but from the Bible, from Isidore of Seville, and from other sources, including a history of the Visigoths in Spain down to the Arab conquest—hence the numerous errors in Ibn Khaldun's quotations from or abbreviation of Orosius's text.[48] Nevertheless, the contribution made by that author to Ibn Khaldun's knowledge of Roman history was immense. That Ibn Khaldun himself thought highly of this source is shown by his preference for the date of the foundation of Rome as given by Orosius (viz., during the reign of Hezekiah, 715–687 B.C.) to that given by Ben Gorion (viz., during the reign of David, 1000–961 B.C.). His reason is that "the authors [wadi'th, "translators"] of the former were two Muslims (sic) who worked as translators for the Muslim caliphs in Cordoba and who are well known."[49]

Josippon

Just as Ibn Khaldun took his information on the Roman Empire from Orosius, he relied on Yosef Ben Gorion, together with the Qur'ān, Old Testament, al-Tabari, al-Mas'udi, and a few other sources, for his knowledge of Jewish history, particularly of the period of the Second Temple.[50] The author of the book in question, known as Josippon, based his book on that of Josephus Flavius (37–95 A.D.), De Bello Judaico, and is believed to have composed his work in southern Italy, at the end of the tenth century. The book was translated into numerous languages, including Arabic, and was read by Ibn Khaldun when he was in Egypt. He used it extensively and quoted it freely, basing on it most of his account of Jewish history. Ibn Khaldun states explicitly that that book was his source for the period between Nebuchadnezzar and Titus, a period neglected by Muslin historians.[51] It may be added that other Arab historians, including Ibn al-'Amīd, used it as a source.

An interesting fact may be noted. Whereas in *al-Muqaddimah* Ibn Khaldun did not revise his account of Roman history in the light of what he had learned from Orosius, yet he added a long passage[52] taken from Ben Gorion and quoted the author's name. This suggests that some revision of *al-Muqaddimah* was made during Ibn Khaldun's stay in Egypt.[53]

Ibn al-'Amīd

The third main source used by Ibn Khaldun for pre-Islamic history was Ibn al-'Amīd al-Makin (1205–1273), on whom he drew for the history of Christianity.[54] Ibn al-'Amīd was an Arabic-speaking Copt whose history, *Lubab al-Tawarikh*, began with Adam and ended in 1260 with the accession of Baybars. It takes the form of biographies down to 586 B.C., then traces the ancient dynasties of Asia, the Hellenistic world, Rome, Byzantium, and Islam. No complete edition of it has yet been published.

Al-Musabbihi

Several of Ibn Khaldun's quotations from Ibn al-'Amīd cite al-Musabbihi as their source, and there are also direct citations of al-Musabbihi.[55] The latter mentions several emperors—including Gaius, Nero, Aurelius, Alexander, whose mother was a Christian (Mammea), Aurelian, and Probus—all of them in connection with Christian persecution. Al-Musabbihi (977–1029) wrote a history of Egypt, *Akhbār Misr,* in about 40 volumes, ending around A.H. (1024/1025).[56] This was used extensively by subsequent historians, including Ibn Khallikan, Ibn Duqmaq, al-Maqrizi, and Ibn Iyas. Most of the work has perished, but volume 40 has recently been edited and published in Cairo.

One last question remains: To what extent could Ibn Khaldun have taken Jewish, Roman, and Christian history and fitted the information he acquired into his basic model? The short answer is: hardly at all.

Jewish history could be dealt with most easily, since Ibn Khaldun seems to have considered the Jews as one more Arab tribe and, until the advent of Jesus, as proto-Muslims! An example is their loss of 'asabiya during their servitude in Egypt. When Moses urged them to go and conquer Syria, "They said: 'there are giants in that country and we shall not enter it until the giants have departed.' That is, until God had driven them out by manifesting his power, without the application of our group feeling, and that will be one of your miracles, O Moses. And when Moses urged them on, they persisted and became rebellious, and said: 'Go you yourself and your Lord, and fight.'"[57]

But after they had spent 40 years in the wilderness, there appeared "another powerful generation that knew neither laws nor oppression and did not have the stigma of meekness. Thus a new group feeling could grow up [in the new generation] and that [new group feeling] enables them to press their claims and to achieve superiority. . . . This shows most clearly what group feeling means."

It is worth noting, however, that in his 46-page account of the history of the Jews in al'Ibar,[58] Ibn Khaldun never introduces either 'asabiya or any other of his basic concepts. Instead, it is a detailed historical chronicle, based mainly on the Qur'ān and the Bible, supplemented by such sources as al-Tabari, Ibn al-'Amīd, Orosius, and Josippon, whose conflicting versions he takes into account. Throughout, he tries to place Jewish history in its wider context, bringing in Assyrian, Babylonian, Egyptian, Persian, and Roman developments.

Ibn Khaldun also failed to apply the concepts he had worked out in al-Muqaddimah to Roman history. Nor did he think that that history necessitated the modification of his basic model. He was aware that the monarchy had been replaced by a republic and that Julius Caesar and his successors ruled as monarchs, but that does not seem to have impressed him greatly. Nor could he discern in Roman history the cyclical patterns he saw so clearly in Arab history. Of course, he was aware that the expansion of Rome was followed by stability and then contraction, with the Gothic, Arab, and Turkish invasions, but he did not attempt to analyze the causes of the decline.

As for the history of Christianity, it must have struck him as puzzling. Here was a religion that for 300 years spread by conversion and did not attempt to gain power by basing itself on a tribal 'asabiya. When it finally became dominant, it did so through the conversion of Emperor Constantine. He must also have been puzzled by the frequency of religious heresies and schisms, phenomena that did not have a Muslim counterpart. In other words, Ibn Khaldun derived his sociological models from his reading of Muslim—or, more precisely, Arab and Berber—history. Perhaps more than any other Muslim historian, except Rashid al-Din, he was interested in the history of non-Muslims as well; but though the study of these people intrigued him as a historian, it did not affect his understanding of the basic laws governing human society.

Medieval European Historians

We can now compare Ibn Khaldun's knowledge of universal history with that of a somewhat earlier Western European, Bishop Otto of Friesing (born ca. 1111–1115; died 1158), an outstanding medieval historian whose "*Chronicle* is the earliest philosophical treatment of history which we have."[59] Like Ibn Khaldun, Otto was not a cloistered scholar but very much a man of the world. Grandson of Emperor Henry IV, nephew of Henry V, half-brother of Conrad III, he was the maternal uncle of Frederick I "Barbarossa," under whom he occupied a high position.[60] He studied philosophy in Paris, filled an important see, knew at least some Greek, was interested in the history of philosophy, and was acquainted with the newly translated works of Aristotle. He traveled to Italy and took part in the Second Crusade, which took him through Hungary and Anatolia and to Jerusalem.[61] No attempt is made here to discuss his philosophy of history or his notion of the Two Cities but only to gauge the extent of his knowledge of world history, as compared with that of Ibn Khaldun.

No medieval European had anything like Ibn Khaldun's geographical knowledge, based as it was on the intense commercial and scientific activity of the vast world of Islam. Unlike Ibn Khaldun, Otto does not begin with a long geographical introduction, and it is clear that his knowledge of the subject is very limited. And, although Ranulf Higden (died 1363; see note 59) begins his book with a lengthy geographical introduction, and his estimate of the size of the earth is fairly accurate (he puts the diameter at 6,491 miles), his account does not cover anything east of India or south of Ethiopia and is full of absurd tales.[62]

Another subject where the Europeans do not begin to match Ibn Khaldun is, naturally, the history of the Arabs and Islam. Otto has exactly two general references to "Saracens": the defeat of Heraclius and "waste of his empire" and the victories of Charles Martel "near Narbonne" and of Liutprand in Provence. But, thanks to his experiences in Anatolia and Palestine during the Second Crusade, he did have some interest in the contemporary Muslim world and gave a fairly extensive account of the negotiations between the Fatimids and Crusaders, a brief description of the two Babylons, Baghdad and Cairo, an account of the capture of Edessa by Zangi, and a brief passage on Prester John.[63] He is also unaware of pre-Islamic Arab or Persian history, but there are references to Crassus' defeat at Carrhae, the victory of Sapor over the Romans, and the defeat of Chosroes by Heraclius.[64]

In contrast, Ibn Khaldun was well informed about pre-Islamic Arabia. He also has a garbled, largely legendary, account of Parthian (Arsacīd, *al-Ashkaniya*) history, which, however, does get the main phases fairly accurately.[65] On the Sassanians (*al-Sasaniya*) Ibn Khaldun is more knowledgeable and devotes no less than 14 pages to their history, based on such authors as Al-Tabai, Hisham ibn al-Kalbi, al-Mas'udi, and Ibn Ishaq.[66] He has an essentially accurate list of the Persian kings (including the two queens, Buran and Azarmid, daughters of Khusru Parviz), sketches of their characters and struggles for power, and an extensive account of their wars with the Romans and with the Turks, Khazars, and other northern peoples. He is well informed on their relations with the Arabs of Kindah and their expansion into the Gulf and Yemen. He even mentions such matters as the suppression of the Mazdakites and Manichaeans, the great famine under Peroz, and the plague, which in 629 A.D. carried off Kavadh Sheroe and "half, or a third of the population."[67]

Otto, however, was, naturally, much better informed on the history of Europe after the fall of Rome. He also had a vastly wider and deeper knowledge of the history of Rome and of Constantinople down to the year 800, when Charlemagne was crowned Emperor and Otto's interest in Byzantine history ceased.

Otto knew much less about the Greeks than about the Romans, and that mainly about the Hellenistic period, when their history was intertwined with that of Rome. However, his information was distinctly greater than that of Ibn Khaldun.

The foregoing is not surprising. It is to be expected that a Christian should have known more about the classical world, which he regarded as part of his history, than did a Muslim, for whom it was alien. What is perhaps more unexpected is that Otto knew more about the preclassical world than did Ibn Khaldun.

First, as regards the Jews. Otto was better informed, because, unlike Ibn Khaldun, he had direct access to the Old Testament. He also drew freely on the works of Josephus, particularly the *Antiquities* and the *Wars*.[68]

Otto devotes quite a few pages to the history of Egypt, and that of Mesopotamia.[69] Almost all repeat the legends that Herodotus—whom he does not cite—and other Greek writers made familiar to the classical world. But it should be noted that he mentions both Manetho, the Egyptian, and Berosus, the Chaldean, whose works on the history of their countries were the most authoritative available in antiquity and fragments of which are to be found in Josephus and Eusebius. On this topic, too, he is far better informed than Ibn Khaldun, who had almost nothing to say about Egypt or Mesopotamia.[70]

But it is on ancient Persian history that the contrast is most striking. Ibn Khaldun devotes a chapter to this subject, but it is very confused.[71] Most of it is taken from the Persian legends on the wars between Iran and Turan, on Rustum and "The Lot / Of Kaikobad and Kaikhosru forgot."

Into this he intersperses short accounts of Jeremiah, Nebuchadnezzar, and the story of Esther. There is, however, one page that gives a coherent account of the Achaemenians, from Cyrus to the Macedonian conquest; significantly, it was taken from Orosius.

Otto, however, has a short—and mainly mythical—account of the Medes and a long, and essentially accurate, one of the Persians, including a list of their kings.[72]

It remains to ask what were the sources that enabled Otto to have a more detailed and accurate understanding of classical and ancient history. These were mainly the great Christian works of late antiquity: the Vulgate and also Eusebius, Jerome, St. Augustine, Orosius, and Justin—works of men who had absorbed most of the Greek and Latin historiography available in antiquity. Moreover, Otto occasionally reaches behind them to such authors as Cicero, Varro, Tacitus, and perhaps—although he does not cite him—Livy, parts of whose works circulated widely in the Middle Ages.

Byzantine Historians

Turning to Byzantium, it would be inappropriate to compare Ibn Khaldun with the more distinguished Byzantine historians, such as Procopius and Psellus, for they covered much shorter periods and did not stretch back to antiquity. We must, therefore, make do with someone who was intellectually much inferior, John Malalas (ca. 490–ca. 570), but who had an adequate knowledge of ancient history.

Malalas, whose chronicle covers the period from Adam to 565 A.D., has often been taken to task—among others, by Gibbon and Bury—for his uncritical use of sources, his credulity, his lack of organization, and other defects.[73] But his knowledge of classical antiquity was quite wide, and he often has a firm grasp of the main events of Macedonian, Roman, and Jewish history. On the Babylonians, Assyrians, Egyptians, and Persians, he repeats the tales told by the Greek historians, but he has one citation from Manetho (but none from Berosus), obviously taken at second hand, "For the period from Zeno [reigned 474–491] onwards [that is, for his lifetime] he [Malalas] claims reliance on oral sources of information."[74] For earlier events, "Malalas had to rely on written records and cites, largely at second hand, numerous Greek and Latin authors, including some that are otherwise unknown."[75] The list of historians cited by Malalas is very long, but most of it is indirect. "Most of the references to the Latin writers are so vague that . . . one is almost compelled to conclude that Malalas' acquaintance with them was second hand. This applies to the references to Florus, Livy, Lucan, Ovid, Pliny, Sallust, Servius and Suetonius Tranquillus."[76] He knew the Greek historians much better and cites Herodotus, Xenophon, Thucydides, Polybius, Diodorus Siculus, Plutarch, Arrian, and others. Among the historians on whom he greatly relied was Eusebius, who, in Byzantium, "remained the major source for the early centuries of Christianity," and Josephus.[77] He also quotes, cites, or mentions such writers and thinkers as Homer, Democritus, Heraclitus, Hippocrates, Socrates, Plato, Aristotle, Sophocles, Euripides, Aristophanes, Demosthenes, Isocrates, and Aeschines.[78] Clearly, whatever his shortcomings, Malalas knew much more about Greco-Roman and Jewish history and distinctly more about preclassical antiquity than did Ibn Khaldun; and he was particularly interested in the Persians.

Broadly speaking, the same may be said of a slightly later and inferior work, the *Chronicon Paschale*, which covers the period 284–628 A.D. It deals with the Chaldeans, Assyrians, Hebrews, Greeks, and Romans and relies heavily on Malalas.[79]

Malalas survived the Dark Ages of Byzantium, the seventh and eighth centuries. He is cited by Theophanes (ca. 760–ca. 818), whose chronicle covers the years 760–818 A.D.[80] Although not mentioned in Photius' *Bibliotheca*, his work was used as a source by later scholars. When Constantine Porphyrogenitus (905–959) had texts excerpted for his historical encyclopedia, Malalas was among the authors selected. Also in the tenth century, "the cycle known as Souda [or Suidas] includes a number of articles that reflect Malalas' text." John Tzetzes (ca. 1110–1180) cited the *Chronicle*, but after the late thirteenth century, it was little used by other scholars. However, Malalas had some influence on Slavic, Syrian, and Latin chronicles.[81]

Meanwhile, Byzantine knowledge of ancient history had greatly expanded. The polymath Photius (ca. 810–893) compiled the *Bibliotheca*, a voluminous set of reviews of books he had read. In the historical section, he has "39 Codices and 31 authors who, with the exception of four, all belong to the imperial or Byzantine period. . . . We see that Photius still read the forty books of Diodorus, Appian's Roman history in its entirety, Arrian's historical works, etc. In all we know twenty historians exclusively through the *Bibliotheca*, and four more in a more complete form thanks to it."[82] Among the older authors, he mentions Herodotus, Theopompus, and Ctesias (the author of books on Persia and India), and he "naturally knew Thucydides and Xenophon." He also cites Plutarch, Josephus, and Eusebius but not Polybius or Posidonius. Among the orators he reviews are Isocrates, Aeschines, and Demosthenes and among the philosophers, Plato and Aristotle.[83] Two more points may be observed. First, "several reviews of historians [codices 63–65 and 72] show an overriding concern with the affairs of the orient," especially the Persians. Secondly, in philosophy, he "had read more widely than the *Bibliotheca* shows."[84]

Another sign of the growing Byzantine interest in ancient history is provided by the spread of Orosius's *History*, "its influence was ubiquitous [approximately 200 MSS survive], being sufficiently regarded" for the Byzantine emperor to send a copy to the Caliph in Spain (see earlier in this chapter).[85]

The expanding range of historical knowledge available to the Byzantines may also be gauged from the *Souda* or *Suidas*, probably written around 1000 A.D.[86] According to De Boor, the following authors were used: Herodotus, Thucydides, Xenophon, Polybius, Diodorus, Dionysius, Josephus, Arrian, Appian, Cassius Dio, Iamblichus, Procopius, and others.

By the thirteenth century, Byzantine scholars had rediscovered Latin literature, and Planudes (ca. 1255–1305) translated works by

Augustine, Ovid, Cicero, Macrobius, Boethius, and at least some lines by Juvenal.[87]

It may therefore be safely stated that the Byzantines knew much more about ancient history than did Western Europeans until the Renaissance or than did the world of Islam until much later. It should be noted, however, that their knowledge of Rome was far smaller than that of Greece. Even a historian like Procopius, who was so close to Imperial Rome in time, knew Latin, and had campaigned in Italy and North Africa, shows little familiarity with Roman history, as contrasted with either Roman mythology or the earlier Hellenic and Hellenistic periods.[88]

A few words may be added on the Byzantines' knowledge of the world they lived in. A good starting point is *De Administrando Imperio*, by the emperor Constantine Porphyrogenitus, written around 962.[89] This book, evidently based on government reports, shows an accurate knowledge of the geography, ethnography, and recent history and politics of the surrounding areas and peoples: Russia as far as Novgorod; the Balkans and Central Europe up to Moravia—including the Croats, Bulgars, Serbs, Pechenegs, Turks, and Khazars—the Caucasus; and Italy. A less firm and detailed knowledge is evident on the Muslim world, from Iraq to Spain. France and the Franks receive attention but not the Holy Roman Empire or the Germans; yet, there must have been some information about the latter, acquired through exchange of ambassadors and royal marriages. Similarly, there is no mention of Persia, which was not at that time an independent state, but much must have been known about it from Procopius and other historians and from information derived from ambassadors and prisoners taken by both sides.

Occasionally, interest in neighboring lands went beyond the political and commercial. Around the middle of the eleventh century, Michael Psellus (1018–1096) had Georgian, Armenian, and Syrian pupils, and there are signs that Arabic astronomy had some influence on Byzantine. His student, John Italus (ca. 1025–d. after 1082), states that Hellenic culture had passed on to the "Assyrians, Medes and Egyptians" [i.e., Arabs and Persians] and that in Susa, Ecbatana, and Babylon [Ahwaz, Hamadan, and Baghdad] "he will hear of things which, despite his Hellenic culture, he had never heard of."[90] In the fourteenth century, there was a large infusion of Muslim science through northwest Iran.[91]

With India, there were fairly close commercial and diplomatic relations under the late Roman Empire. Cosmos Indicopleustes, writing in the first half of the sixth century, gives much information on that country. The Arab conquest, however, severed these contacts, and legends gradually replaced the earlier knowledge.[92]

There was also contact with China through the Silk Route, and the story of the smuggling of silkworms to Constantinople by Nestorian monks under Justinian may well be true. The Mongol conquests reopened these routes, and Chinese Nestorians visited Constantinople, enroute to Western Europe, around 1286. But information about China remained scarce.[93]

Of course, strictly speaking, neither Ibn Khaldun nor the Western Europeans and Byzantines deserve the title of "universal historians," since they knew so little of the histories of India and China. There was only one universal historian before modern times, Rashid al-Din, whose position as vizier in the vast Mongol empire gave him access to all the major civilizations and whose great intellectual curiosity made him draw on Chinese, Indian, and Latin, as well as on European, Muslim, and Jewish, sources and informants.

CONCLUSION

The conclusion may be stated very briefly. Ibn Khaldun knew much more about the world in which he lived than did his European or Byzantine contemporaries, and he had a much wider and deeper knowledge of Islamic and, possibly, of late Persian history. But of classical and preclassical history he knew very little. As a social scientist he is worthy to stand alongside Plato, Aristotle, and Thucydides, and his thought was unequaled in the 2,000 years between Aristotle and the seventeenth century. But in historiography, genius is no substitute for information, and a river cannot rise above its sources. Ibn Khaldun paid the price for the selective interest taken by the Arabs in Greek culture. They understood the importance and utility of Greek mathematics, science, medicine, and philosophy, absorbed them, and produced great ones of their own. But they ignored Greek and Latin politics, art, drama, literature, and historiography. As a result, they remained ignorant not only of the classical world but of the earlier civilizations. It is significant that the Greek word *historia* became the Arabic *ustura* (legend), historiography being *tarikh*. Of course, most Muslims (but not Ibn Khaldun) would have rejoined that the history of these civilizations had nothing to teach them!

I should like to end this chapter with a plea. So far, interest in Ibn Khaldun has concentrated almost entirely on *al-Muqaddimah*. However, as this chapter has tried to show,[94] there is much in *al-'Ibar* that sheds light on other aspects of his thinking and knowledge. It would, therefore, be highly desirable if some younger scholars took up the task of editing, translating, and studying *al-'Ibar*; after all, both books were the product of the same great mind.

Notes

I am indebted to Professors William Jordan, Bernard Lewis, and Franz Rosenthal, and Jane Baun, a graduate student at Princeton, for many helpful comments and references.

1. Franz Rosenthal, *The Muqaddimah* (New York, 1958), vol. 1, p. 57. All references to the *Muqaddimah* are to this translation. I have read the Arabic text of the *Muqaddimah* and relevant parts of the *'Ibar*.

2. Ibid., 1, p. 78.

3. Ibid., 2, pp. 287–88.

4. Ibid., 3, pp. 131–51. Ibn Khaldun also states that the main Greek mathematicians were skilled carpenters (2, p. 365).

5. Ibid., 3, p. 412. In the eighth century, partial Arabic translations of the *Iliad* and *Odyssey* circulated in Baghdad; see Gustave von Grunebaum, *Medieval Islam* (Chicago, 1946), p. 303, and Sulayman al-Bustani, *Iliadhat Humerus* (Cairo, 1904), pp. 36–38.

6. Ibid., 2, pp. 266, 326.

7. Ibid., 3, pp. 113–14.

8. Ibid., 1, pp. 73, 162. The reference to the "great wall" is almost certainly to the Great Wall of China.

9. Ibid., 1, p. 298.

10. Ibid., 3, p. 115.

11. Ibid., 3, p. 284.

12. Ibid., 3, pp. 476–77.

13. Ibid., 3, p. 185.

14. Ibid., 2, p. 288.

15. Ibid., 2, p. 350.

16. Ibid., 2, p. 266.

17. Ibid., 1, pp. 330, 333; 2, p. 319.

18. Ibid., 2, p. 38.

19. Ibid., 1, p. 357; see also 2, p. 239.

20. Ibid., 2, p. 241.

21. Ibid., 2, p. 319.

22. Ibid., 1, p. 305.

23. Ibid., 2, p. 287.

24. Ibid., 1, pp. 473–78.

25. Ibid., 1, pp. 478–81.

26. Ibid., 2, pp. 261–62.

27. Ibid., 1, p. 479. See also, Franz Rosenthal, "The Influence of the Biblical Tradition on Muslim Historiography," in Bernard Lewis and P. M. Holt (eds.), Historians of the Middle East (London, 1962), pp. 35–45.

28. References are to Tarikh Ibn Khaldun, Beirut edition, 1391/1971, published by al-A'lami Press, in seven volumes (all quotations are translated by me). The text is not satisfactory, and one must presume that many of the errors in it are due to copyists or printers; see, on this subject, al-Bustani, op. cit., pp. 80–81. For Ibn Khaldun's interest in non-Muslim history, see Mohamed Talbi, Ebn Haldun et l'Histoire (Tunis, 1973), pp. 112–14.

29. Alan E. Samuel, Greek and Roman Chronology (Munich, 1972).

30. Tarikh, pp. 184–95.

31. Ibid., 2, pp. 116–27.

32. Ibid., 2, pp. 196–97.

33. Ibid., 2, pp. 197–98.

34. Ibn Khaldun was, of course, not aware that Hannibal's name consisted of two Semitic words, which he probably would have had no difficulty in recognizing!

35. Ibid., 2, pp. 198–210.

36. Ibid., 2, pp. 210–23.

37. Ibid., 2, pp. 223–34.

38. Ibid., 2, pp. 234–36.

39. Ibid., 2, part 2, pp. 105–6.

40. Ibid., 6, pp. 106–8; French translation by Baron W. McG. De Slane, Histoire des Berbères, new edition by Paul Casanova (Paris 1925), vol. 1, pp. 206–10.

41. Muqaddimah, 1, p. 47.

42. Muhammad T. al-Tanji, al-Ta'rif bi Ibn Khaldun (Cairo, 1951), p. 229.

43. There are two English translations of Orosius: Irving W. Raymond, Seven Books of History Against the Pagans (New York, 1936) and Roy J. Deferrari, The Seven Books of History Against the Pagans (Washington, D.C., 1964).

44. See Giorgio Levi Della Vida, "La Traduzione araba delle Storie di Orosio," Al Andalus (Madrid), vol. 19, fasc. 2, 1954. This article is criticized by Abd al-Rahman Badawi, Awrusius, Tarikh al-'Alam (Beirut, 1982). I wrote the first draft of this chapter before I had access to this book.

45. There are, of course, scattered references to Rome and Roman history, especially where it impinged on Hellenistic or Jewish history. See, for example, Ibn al-Qifti, Tarikh al-Hukama (Leipzig, 1893); Sa'id al-Andalusi, Tabaqat al-umam (Cairo, n.d.); and extracts in Franz Rosenthal, Das Fortleben der Antike in Islam (Zürich and Stuttgart, 1965). At the other end

of the Muslim world, Rashid al-Din (ca. 1247–1318), noted physician and vizier of Ghazan Khan, wrote a monumental world history, *Jami' al-Tawarikh*. There is no complete edition; see the Persian text and partial Russian translation, *Fazllah Rashid al-Din, Dzhami at Tavarikh*, 3 vols. (Baku, 1957; Moscow, 1965, 1980). This volume covers the Mongols, Jews, Muslims, Persians, Turks, Chinese, Indians, and Franks. The part on the Franks includes a description of Europe and a historical account of Roman, Christian, and European history, starting with the birth of Christ and ending in 705 A.H. (1305–1306 A.D.). Thanks to Rashid al-Din's European informants, and to the Latin sources they used, he has somewhat more information on the period between Augustus and Heraclius—especially on the popes—than does Ibn Khaldun. For Persian text and annotated translation, see Karl Jahn, *Histoire universelle de Rasid al-Din*, 1, *Histoire des Francs* (Leiden, 1951); idem, *Die Frankengeschichte des Raschid al-Din* (Vienna, 1977); also idem, "Universalgeschichte im Islamischen Raum," *Mensch und Weltgeschichte* (Salzburg and Munich, 1969), pp. 145–70.

46. A few other Arabs occasionally quote Orosius; for example, Ibn Juljul, *Tarikh al-hukama wa al-attiba* (written in 987/988), the geographers al-Bakri (died 1094) and Muhammad al-Himyari (died 1326/1327), al-Maqrizi (died 1423), who used passages not found in Ibn Khaldun, and the author of an anonymous *Tarikh*—see Badawi, op. cit., pp. 21–35.

47. Raymond, op. cit., pp. 5, 15.

48. For a critical analysis of Ibn Khaldun's use of Orosius, which is mainly a free and abbreviated adaptation, see Badawi, op. cit., pp. 35–47.

49. *'Ibar*, 2, p. 197.

50. The following account is based on Walter J. Fischel, "Ibn Khaldun and Josippon," *Homenaje a Millas-Vallicrosa* (Barcelona, 1954), pp. 587–98; see also idem, "Ibn Khaldun: On the Bible, Judaism and the Jews," *Ignace Goldziher Memorial*, vol. 2 (Jerusalem, 1956), pp. 147–71; idem, "Ibn Khaldun's Activities in Mamluk Egypt," *Semitic and Oriental Studies Presented to William Popper* (Berkeley and Los Angeles, 1951), pp. 103–24; Meyer Waxman, *A History of Jewish Literature* (New York and London, 1960), vol. 1, pp. 419–21; and Moritz Steinschneider, *Die Geschichtsliteratur der Juden* (Frankfurt, 1905), pp. 28–32.

51. *'Ibar*, 2, p. 116.

52. *Muqaddimah*, p. 477, in Rosenthal translation.

53. For the successive revisions of *al-Muqaddimah*, see Rosenthal, op. cit., vol. 1, pp. civ–cvii.

54. See *Encyclopedia of Islam*, 2nd edition, s.v. Al-Makin, Ibn Al-'Amīd; G. Graff, *Geschichte der Christlichen arabische Literatur* (Vatican, 1947), vol. 2, pp. 348–51.

55. See, for example, *'Ibar*, 2, pp. 201, 205, 206, 208, 214.

56. Ayman Fuad Sayyid and Thierry Bianquis, *Akhbar Misr* (Cairo, 1978; Institut français d'archéologie orientale du Caire).

57. Rosenthal, 1, pp. 287–88; the quotations are from the Qur'ān.

58. *'Ibar*, 2, pp. 81–127.

59. *The Two Cities: A Chronicle of Universal History to the Year 1146* A.D., translated by Charles C. Mierow and edited by Austin P. Evans and Charles Knapp (New York, 1928), p. 4; all references are to this edition. I have also read, for comparative purposes, *The Ecclesiastical History of Orderic Vitalis*, edited by Marjorie Chibnall (Oxford, 1980), six volumes; Ranulf Higden, *Polychronicon*, edited by Churchill Babington (London, 1865–1886; reprint Nendeln/Liechtenstein, 1975), nine volumes; and *John Capgrave Abbreviacion of Cronicles*, edited by Peter J. Lucas (Oxford, 1983). These books were suggested to me by my colleague William Jordan.

60. *Two Cities*, op. cit., p. 17.

61. *Two Cities*, op. cit., pp. 12–14, 39–44.

62. Higden, op. cit., vol. 1, p. 40, passim.

63. Freising, op. cit., pp. 338, 344, 407–10, 439–44.

64. Ibid., pp. 213, 287, 336.

65. *'Ibar*, op. cit., pp. 167–69.

66. Ibid., pp. 169–82.

67. Ibid., p. 181.

68. Freising, op. cit., p. 26.

69. Ibid., pp. 131–52.

70. Part of Manetho's king-list, derived from the summary by Eusebius, appears in Biruni's *Athar* and Maqrizi's *Khitat*—see Michael Cook, "Pharaonic History in Medieval Egypt," *Studia Islamica*, fasc. 57, 1983.

71. *'Ibar*, pp. 159–67.

72. Freising, op. cit., pp. 154–56, 165–82, the latter interspersed with Greek and Roman history.

73. *The Chronicles of John Malalas*, translated by Elizabeth Jeffreys, et al. (Melbourne, 1986).

74. Ibid., pp. xxii–xxiii.

75. Loc. cit.

76. Elizabeth Jeffreys et al., *Studies in John Malalas* (Sydney, 1990), p. 38.

77. *Oxford Dictionary of Byzantium* (New York, 1991), s.v. "Eusebius," "Josephus."

78. For a list of the authors cited by Malalas and the sources to which he had direct or indirect access, see Jeffreys, *Studies*, op. cit., pp. 172–97.

79. *Chronicon Paschale, 284–628* A.D., translated with notes and introduction by Michael Whitby and Mary Whitby (Liverpool, 1989).

80. Jeffreys, *Studies*, op. cit., p. 257; but he does not appear in the index of H. Turtledove, *The Chronicle of Theophanes* (Philadelphia, 1982).

81. Ibid., pp. 257–62.

82. Paul Lemerle, *Byzantine Humanism* (Canberra, 1986), p. 225.

83. Pauly-Wissowa, *Real Encyclopädie* (Stuttgart, 1941), s.v. "Photios."

84. N. G. Wilson, *Scholars of Byzantium* (Baltimore, 1983), pp. 100–101.

85. A. A. Mosshammer, *The Chronicle of Eusebius and Greek Chronographic Tradition* (Lewisburg, Penn., 1979).

86. *Oxford Dictionary of Byzantium*, op. cit., s.v. "Souda"; F. Pauly-Wissowa, op. cit., s.v. "Suidas."

87. *Oxford Dictionary of Byzantium*, op. cit., s.v. "Planudes," Wilson, op. cit., pp. 230–41.

88. J. A. S. Evans, *Procopius* (New York, 1972), pp. 101–2.

89. Constantine Porphyrogenitus, *De Administrando Imperio*, translated and edited by G. Moravcsik, R. J. H. Jenkins, et al., two volumes (Budapest, 1949; London, 1962).

90. Wilson, op. cit., pp. 148–66.

91. H. W. Haussig, *A History of Byzantine Civilization* (New York, 1971), pp. 326–27.

92. *Oxford Dictionary of Byzantium*, op. cit., s.v. "India," "Kosmas Indiko-pleustes."

93. Ibid., s.v. "China," "Silk Route."

94. I now realize that my methodology in this chapter is outdated. It should have begun: "The deconstruction of Ibn Khaldun's discourse reveals a *mentalité* structure based on a sexist patriarchal hegemony, ethnic arrogance, gender dominance, and economic exploitation. It is intended to mystify and marginalize the masses and impede their empowerment. The text and subtext should therefore be thoroughly decoded, critiqued, and demystified." And so on.

FIVE

THE OTTOMAN ECONOMIC
LEGACY

Very little work has been done on the subject of the Ottoman legacy in the field of economics, and what I say must be regarded as highly tentative. Much of it will also be critical. Other contributors have drawn attention to the great Ottoman achievements. An empire that lasted six centuries and under which a host of nationalities and religious groups lived, most of the time, in reasonable harmony, is something to admire and praise. Unfortunately, my assigned topic is economics, and economics never was the strong suit of the Ottomans.

My approach is, further, confined to a comparative approach of the Ottoman lands with neighboring Europe. I am not talking about China, of which I know little, or India, of which I know even less. Between them they have accounted for almost half of the world's population and have represented, at various times, the peak of human achievement. What I am saying applies to the lands west of them, the Middle East (including North Africa) and Europe with its offshoots in the New World. And for this portion of humanity I return to the good old eighteenth-century view, which claims that there is a continuous process that can best be represented by a rising line, with numerous breaks and setbacks.[1]

Of the generally agreed-upon constituent elements of a civilization—religion, art, literature, philosophy, natural science, learning, and technology—I will address only the last three. My reasons are twofold. First, because I believe these, and more particularly technology, constitute the main thrust that has pushed humanity from one stage of economic development to the next. Second, they are cumulative: the discoveries of one generation can be handed over to the next, which can than build upon them, though this often fails to occur. They have one thing in common: they represent the application of man's mind to fields in which, because it can work on large amounts of empirical data, human reason seems to operate most efficiently and to yield cumulative results. To a large extent statistics, and to a lesser extent economic theory, share this characteristic, with results I shall discuss later. If Kant had not preempted the term for a very different use, one could have called this activity "practical reason."

One can contrast these activities with religion, and perhaps with art, which in many ways are the finest flowers that humanity has produced. In those fields, the human mind, at an early date, reached dazzling heights and came up against barriers that have, so far, proved insurmountable. In particular, the higher religions reached peaks that have never been surpassed: Hinduism, Zoroastrianism, Buddhism, Judaism, Christianity, Islam. Each of them, in its way, glimpsed an important aspect of the ultimate reality we call God. All are, in their way, valid. And each has witnessed rises and declines in its carrier society and therefore presumably cannot be the major operating factor. Thus, it is absurd to blame Islam for the decline of the Middle East since that region had reached a peak precisely under Islam, in the eighth to twelfth centuries.[2]

My main point is that in the early Middle Ages, the Middle East was *the* center of civilization (not to overlook the magnificent Tang and Sung dynasties but, as already stated, I am not discussing China). After that the center of civilization moved to Europe, and has remained there, and in Europe's American offshoots, ever since. In the fields of science, technology, and economic development, the main legacy of the Ottomans, and of their predecessors the Mamluks and others, was that they cut off the Middle East from the vivifying effects of close contacts with Europe. Hence, the deplorable state of these lands, particularly the Asian parts, toward the end of the eighteenth century when their modern history begins. At that time, they were, by any acceptable economic, social, or cultural criteria, far behind not only Europe and North America but Latin America, Russia, Japan, and possibly China.[3]

In the nineteenth century, Europe, in the form of economic and political imperialism, did indeed impinge on the Middle East with a bang, pushing it forward but also injuring and distorting it, but that, too, is outside my present inquiry.[4]

The discussion that follows will briefly compare Ottoman science and technology with that of contemporary Europe and then treat economic theory, economic organization, and economic policy in both areas.

SCIENCE AND TECHNOLOGY

The rise and high noon of the Ottoman Empire coincides with that of European science: the fifteenth-century precursors, Henry the Navigator and Leonardo; the sixteenth-century pioneers, Copernicus and Vesalius; the seventeenth-century giants, Galileo and Harvey; and so on to Newton and Leibnitz.

And what of the Ottoman Empire? Mehmet II reorganized the *madrasas*, greatly improving the teaching of mathematics, astronomy, and medicine. Under his successors, progress was made in geography and cartography and in 1579 an observatory, as good as those of Europe, was built in Istanbul. A good example of Ottoman science at its best was Taqi al-Din, an astronomer, clockmaker, and inventor of various machines.[5] Around 1565 he wrote a treatise on mechanical clocks.[6] But in all these fields, except cartography, the traditional Muslim methods and books continued to be used and nothing was learned from contemporary Europe, except by a few Jews, Armenians, and Greeks who went to Italy for study. Moreover the various centers soon relapsed into mediocrity and the observatory was actually destroyed at the monarch's order, because of some unfortunate astrological predictions! It was not until the second half of the eighteenth and early nineteenth centuries that the Ottomans began to pick up the rudiments of Western science.[7]

The situation in the Arab provinces was even worse than in the capital.[8] The lingering effect of this unfortunate legacy is illustrated by the backward state of the natural sciences today, in spite of the vigorous efforts of the last 60 to 70 years, in the course of which tens of thousands of students have been sent abroad. According to UNESCO's *Statistical Yearbook*,[9] the most recent estimated number of potential scientists and engineers in Turkey was 14 per thousand of the population, in Lebanon 11, and in Egypt 10; in both Iraq and Syria it was under 3. These figures are of course far below those for Japan (58) as well as Europe and North America, though they compare well with some other third world countries, such as Ecuador 5 and Chile 6. But they are well below those for the Balkan countries: Greece 33, Bulgaria 26, and Yugoslavia 22.

TECHNOLOGY

We can now survey some of the leading aspects of technological activity, starting with agriculture which, in the Middle East as elsewhere, employed at least 80 percent of the population.

Agriculture

The best single indicator of agricultural technology is the yield to seed ratio of wheat, since wheat was by far the predominant crop in both Europe and the Middle East. Ashtor puts the ratio in medieval Egypt at 10 and contrasts it with 2–2.5 in Western Europe in Carolingian times; Bolshakov accepts these figures and believes that Syrian yields were 1.5 times those of Europe, or say 3–4.[10] The latter figure *may* also apply to medieval Anatolia. In the mid-nineteenth century, figures for Turkey and Syria were about 5–6; for Egypt yields were estimated at 14–15 by Napoleon's experts in 1800.[11] The Turkish and Syrian figures compare favorably with those for most European countries in the sixteenth to eighteenth centuries, but are distinctly lower than those for the nineteenth.

Considering that, except in Egypt, natural conditions are much less favorable in the Middle East, and that the agricultural revolution in Europe took place in the eighteenth century or later, one can say that, in this field, the Ottoman Empire did not suffer appreciably from its isolation until quite recently. It may be added that the American crops introduced into Europe—maize, potatoes, and tobacco—found their way to the Middle East quite early. An important Ottoman legacy in agriculture was the land tenure system and the Land Law of 1858 and other nineteenth-century legislation. It was not, however, conducive to economic development.[12]

Mining, Metallurgy, and Armaments

The Ottomans, like other governments, were not terribly interested in agriculture, but they were very much so in mining, metallurgy, and armaments, which provided the sinews of war.

In all these fields, from the fifteenth century onward, Europe was technologically more advanced and innovative than the Ottoman Empire. Examples include the amalgamation process for silver, the use of blast furnaces for iron smelting, and the introduction and spread of water-driven machinery to crush ores and drain mines.[13]

The Ottomans tried hard to keep up with these developments by employing German and other experts to exploit their numerous mines. "They used the mining technique familiar to them in Germany, and even the laws regulating these Ottoman mines were the Saxon mining laws. These are extant in a Turkish version known as Kanuni-Sas, the Saxon Law."[14] Because of their isolation, however, the Ottomans tended to fall increasingly behind; in 1807 Thornton stated: "They call in no foreign assistance to work their mines,"[15] and by the early nineteenth century European observers were all reporting on the poor conditions of the Anatolian mines. A Hungarian expert working for the Ottoman government reported in 1836: "These mines are all in a deplorable state. They are run with great ignorance and therefore at considerable expense."[16]

When it came to firearms, the Ottomans made every effort to keep abreast of Europe, hiring experts (many of them converts to Islam), where necessary. Hence, "as late as 1683, some contemporary Austrian observers noted that the Turkish muskets were as good as those of the Austrians and, in some respects, in range for instance, better."[17] However, as early as 1592, "The Ottoman cannon, though often well cast, are described in Christian sources as ponderous and difficult to move, even with large teams of buffalo and oxen."[18] By 1794 the British ambassador rated the foundries as poor: "The Ottoman Empire never possessed more than two furnaces for casting cannons and mortars (of brass only) . . . and a third for iron shot and shells, all situated in Constantinople."[19] Even the overwhelming interest of the Ottomans in warfare did not allow them to keep up with European technology, which was the offspring of a different society and organization.

Shipbuilding techniques also failed to keep up with those of Europe and by the end of the eighteenth century the Ottomans were importing both warships and merchantships from the United States, Sweden, and elsewhere.[20]

One more point on this subject is relevant to the successor states. Minerals are very scarce in the Arab countries, but in one immensely important field Ottoman law had a great impact: oil. In Muslim law, as in Roman, and in contrast to Anglo-Saxon, subsoil resources belong to the state, not to the owner of the soil. Hence, the Middle Eastern oil industry developed under the system of concessions granted by the state to a company, and not by bilateral contracts between the owner of the soil and the concessionaire, as, say, in Texas. This permitted the development of fields as a unit and, together with favorable geological conditions, explains the phenomenal productivity of the wells and very high profitability of the industry.

Textiles

The Middle East's preeminence in textiles is shown by such loan words as damask, gauze, taffeta, and many others. However, according to Ashtor, already by the fourteenth century "most Near Eastern industries were no longer able to compete with Western manufactured goods, imported by Italian and other merchants."[21] By the thirteenth century the virtual monopoly in silk fabrics enjoyed by the Muslims in Europe had been broken, and by the fifteenth Italian fabrics were selling in the Levant. So were woolen goods. Middle Eastern cotton cloth exports to Europe expanded rapidly in the seventeenth and eighteenth centuries, but were then hit by protective tariffs. By the nineteenth century machine-made textiles poured into the region, and many handicrafts were wiped out, though others managed to struggle on. Instead of being an exporter of manufactures, in the early modern period, and more particularly in the nineteenth century, the Middle East became an exporter of raw textile materials, particularly silk, cotton, and, for some time, flax. It was only at the end of the nineteenth century that modern textile factories were established in Turkey and Egypt.[22]

Paper and Printing

A paper mill was set up in Baghdad in 751, allegedly by Chinese prisoners captured at the battle of Talas. From there it spread to Byzantium and westward to Europe, and in the Middle Ages, Middle Eastern exports to Europe were very large. By the sixteenth century, however, the bulk of Istanbul's consumption was met by European imports, though there was some local manufacture.[23]

The Arabs eagerly accepted Chinese paper, but not Chinese printing. In the sixteenth century Arabic books were printed in Italy and, in the following century, in other European countries. But in 1485 Sultan Bayazit II imposed a ban on the possession of printed matter in Arabic or Turkish, and this was confirmed by Selim I in 1515. It did not apply to Hebrew, Armenian, or Greek books, and presses in these languages were soon set up, as were others, also by Christians, in Syria and Lebanon. It was only in the eighteenth century that printing in Turkish began and, as Şerif Mardin points out, even then it encountered much opposition.[24]

Mechanical Power

Before the invention of steam engines, mechanical power meant watermills and windmills. Both were invented in the Middle East, the watermill at the beginning of the Christian era and the windmill in the sixth century, but neither was much used in the region—the watermill because of the lack of suitable streams and the windmill for no obvious reason.

But both were greatly improved and widely used in Europe. In England in 1086, the Doomsday Book shows that there was one watermill for every 195 inhabitants. This may be contrasted with the situation in the Middle East five centuries later. The corresponding figures were 326 in Tokat, 460 in Malatya, and 1,424 in Safad, though the last figure may be due to an undercount of mills. In the rest of Syria, and in Iraq, Egypt, and Arabia, there were very few mills. Two more points may be noted: first, the power of the watermills represented a substantial addition to the labor force—in England at least one third. Second, there were nearly two watermills for every English village, most of which were very small, which means that practically everyone was familiar with the machinery of the mill and with various attachments such as cams and cranks; watermills were used for a wide variety of industrial processes.[25]

The contrast was even more striking with windmills. In the flatter parts of Europe, where there was little waterpower, such as the Netherlands and eastern England, they played an enormously important role. In the Middle East, however, they went out of use in the Middle Ages. "A French traveler who visited Egypt in 1512 says explicitly that in this country there [were] neither water mills nor windmills" and al-Jabarti mentions those put up by the French in Cairo as an unfamiliar phenomenon. In Palestine, where windmills had been introduced by German crusaders, a few mills were set up in the eighteenth century.[26] Inadequate use of mechanical power was one of the main causes of the relative retardation of the Middle East, and the advent of steam, which began to be used for industrial purposes in England around 1700, greatly widened the gap.

ECONOMICS

This may be studied under three headings: economic practice, economic theory, and economic policy.[27]

Economic Practice

To document adequately the difference in economic practices between Europe and the Ottoman Empire would require the writing of the economic history of the two areas over several centuries. Here only a few points may be noted.

First of all, Muslim law does not recognize the existence of corporate entities. This meant that joint-stock companies could not be formed to carry out large-scale enterprises, as they were in Europe. Of course Islam had many kinds of partnerships, including the *mudaraba*, under which different partners provided capital and enterprise, but these were very seldom of either large size or long duration.[28] The closest approximation to a corporation was the *waqf*, and although *waqfs* occasionally engaged in commercial activities,[29] they were a poor substitute since the vast majority were notoriously mismanaged.

Second, the prohibition of *riba*, though it never stopped lending or usury,[30] must have inhibited the development of banking and stock exchanges. In much of Europe, these institutions developed rapidly in the sixteenth and seventeenth centuries and managed to tap large savings. As a result, interest rates on government loans fell dramatically, to 6 percent in England after 1651, 4 percent in Holland in the 1660s, and 1.5 percent in Genoa after 1664.[31] For comparison, the U.S. government is now paying 6–7 percent and most European governments more—these high figures are, of course, largely due to inflation.

In the Ottoman Empire, on the other hand, the closest approximation to banks were the Galata *sarrafs* who exchanged currencies, granted loans, and discounted various receivables, but do not seem to have taken deposits. Interest rates were seldom below 25 to 30 percent, and often more. It was not until 1856 that the Ottoman Bank was founded, by foreign capital, and a stock exchange was established only in 1873 and led a rather anemic existence.[32] In Egypt modern banks and stock exchanges were established at about the same time and proved more vigorous.

Insurance was another field in which Europe forged ahead. Marine insurance goes back to the fourteenth century and fire insurance was practiced a little later; life insurance goes back to at least the sixteenth century, but was not put on a sound basis until the establishment of life tables at the end of the seventeenth century.[33] But as late as 1851 the British ambassador complained about "the impossibility of insuring houses and property in Constantinople against the risk of fire." Foreign insurance companies then opened branches in the main Ottoman cities and Egypt, but as late as 1900 only one was operating in Baghdad, a Swiss firm that undertook maritime insurance.[34]

Lastly, there is the question of accounting. After the introduction of double-entry bookkeeping, in the late thirteenth or early fourteenth centuries, European methods of accounting became increasingly superior to those of the Middle East. The latter acquired modern accountancy only in the last hundred years or so, when it was introduced by foreign banks and other firms.

Economic Theory and Statistics

Europe's great achievement in theory was to conceive of the economy as a self-regulating mechanism obeying definite and understandable laws. This was first achieved in monetary theory, with Copernicus (1526), Jean Bodin, and others formulating early versions of the Quantity Theory and Gresham's Law. The connection between money and the balance of trade was extensively debated by the mercantilists and by Locke, Cantillon, and others. Hume achieved a fine theoretical synthesis linking money and foreign trade and Adam Smith (1776), in addition to many other contributions, elaborated the notion of division of labor and free trade. Ricardo's *Principles* (1817) finally set economic theory on the path it was to pursue.[35]

A parallel development took place in the field of statistics: from the Middle Ages onward, Europe has always been interested in numbers, in counting men and things.[36] By the sixteenth century this activity had been systematized; "a large part of the work of the Spanish *politicos*, for example, consisted in the collection and interpretation of statistical figures—not to mention the English econometricians, who were called political arithmeticians, and their fellow workers in France, Germany, and Italy."[37]

Among the English, the foremost name is that of Sir William Petty, who has been called by Marx "the founder of political economy." In his *Political Arithmetic* (c. 1672) Petty writes: "Instead of using only comparative and superlative words and intellectual arguments, I have taken the course . . . to express myself in terms of *number, weight,* or *measure*" and he applied his method to various problems. His younger contemporary Gregory King made a careful estimate of the national income and produced an econometric study of the demand for wheat. Petty's friend and collaborator John Graunt worked on the London Bills of Mortality, starting the scientific study of demography and producing Life Tables. The Swiss Jacques Bernouilli developed the theory of probability in 1713. By 1786 the first economic graphs had made their appearance and in 1798 Evelyn had produced an index number for prices.[38]

Turning to the Middle East, in economic thought, as in the other social sciences, Ibn Khaldun towers above his contemporaries, whether Muslim or European.[39] His student al-Maqrizi also shows an understanding of economics and in his *ighathat al-umma bi-kashf al-ghumma* (The Succor of the Nation by Revealing the Misfortune) and his *shudhur al 'uqud fi dhikr al nuqud* (The Fragments of Necklace on the Subject of Coins) gives a very good analysis of the currency debasement and inflation that Egypt was undergoing. After that, however, there was very little progress. Cemal Kafadar's excellent thesis gives a thorough analysis of the economic thought of the leading Ottoman historians at the end of the sixteenth century.[40]

Faced with a sharp rise in prices, these authors could think of only one cause: the debasement of coinage that had been going on since the mid-fifteenth century, to which some added royal extravagance. This was correct, as far as it went, but took no account of the influx of silver from the New World which they, like European bullionists, welcomed. Their remedy was essentially price control. As Kafadar put it: "Our writers were frustrated by the uncontrollable rise of market forces. . . . [R]ather than coming to terms with these forces, they reasserted the primacy of politics which would not allow these forces to play an influential role."[41]

A further check is provided by the writings of the Ottoman bureaucrat Mustafa Ali (1541–1600), who has been described as "one of the most significant intellectual figures of the sixteenth century." And: "Ali was an important member of a group of relatively highly placed intellectuals who were gravely concerned over the course their society seemed to be taking in the late sixteenth century, when rapid changes struck economic, political and social structures all at once." And: "Mustafa Ali achieved posthumous fame largely by virtue of his tremendous historical output and his outspoken social and political critiques."[42]

I carefully read Mustafa Ali's *Counsel for Sultans* in translation,[43] and can affirm that it does not contain one economic thought worth noting or one that shows the kind of understanding to be found in Ibn Khaldun or sixteenth-century European writers.[44] Among the commonplace suggestions it contains are provisions should be laid up against possible shortages; accurate figures should be kept on resources; the migration of lower class yokels ("Turks") to Istanbul should be discouraged by taxation; the public treasury should be protected against waste; the tyranny of the *beglerbeys* over fiscal agents should be curbed; the mixing of ranks should be stopped; provinces should not be subdivided; the currency should not be debased; bribes should be prohibited; standard prices should be set; arrears of taxes should be collected; salaries of soldiers guarding fortresses should be paid; and so on.[45]

I also read his description of Cairo.[46] It contains numerous observations on the manners and customs of Egyptian men and women, usually not flattering, including: "The despotical behavior of most of their governors is caused by their Pharaonization from drinking the water of the Nile" (p. 45). But only two significant economic observations are made. First "the absolute chaos of business life. In every shop several price rates prevail" (p. 44), a state of affairs to be remedied by regulation (p. 80). Second, in his appendix he points out that Egyptians are gravely overtaxed, and the country is consequently declining (p. 80). Clearly, economics was not one of Mustafa Ali's main concerns.

In the seventeenth century, Koçu Bey, writing in 1630, and Katib Çelebi, around 1653, showed no greater understanding of economic matters, and the historian Naima took very little interest in them. Nor did the Egyptian historian al-Jabarti, until the Napoleonic invasion turned his world upside down.[47]

Passing on to statistics, one is struck by the low degree of numeracy of the Ottomans, as of their predecessors. It is not merely that their often good mathematicians took no interest in statistical theory or application but that their writers so seldom used numbers.[48] The wide range of figures which enabled Gregory King to estimate the national income, and which are so frequently used by Adam Smith to illustrate a point, were simply not available in the

Middle East. As far as I am aware, no one bothered to look into the abundant data in the *defters*, add up the figures and use them. I should be surprised to learn that any Ottoman statesman knew the approximate population of the empire, much less its production of wheat or its shipping—though it is possible that a discovery in the archives will prove me completely wrong. Of course they knew the number of soldiers, and the tax and other revenues, and when necessary checked the available figures. Thus, in 931 A.H. (1524/25) "detailed lists were prepared . . . that compare the populations of each wage-receiving/[military] unit in 917 . . . in 926 . . . and in 931." This was prepared for the "Head Measurer who had been brought from Egypt by Selim I and appointed to work at the Treasury because of his mathematical skills."[49]

Economic Policy

One should start with a significant fact: the Ottoman rulers lived within their means to a much greater degree than most of the European states, and bankruptcies—such as those of the Hapsburgs—were unknown. It is also possible that, in the sixteenth to eighteenth centuries, the Ottoman taxes were much lighter than European. If the figures given by Stratford Canning in 1809 are to be trusted, the amount reaching the government was only £2,250,000 (much more must have been collected), compared to £17 million in Great Britain and £24 million in France.[50]

At this point a quotation from David MacPherson, writing in 1805, is apt: "No judicious commercial regulations could be drawn up by ecclesiastical or military men (the only classes who possessed any authority or influence) who despised trade and consequently could know nothing of it."[51] MacPherson had medieval European governments in mind, but his judgment applies even more to Middle Eastern governments.

In these, the dominant elements were bureaucrats and soldiers, whose interest in economic matters was limited to taxation and provisioning. Taxes supplied the revenues needed to defray the expenses of the court, the army, and the bureaucracy, and it is not surprising that almost the only statistics available in Arabic and Turkish writings are army lists and tax returns. Provisioning applied to the cities, whose inhabitants could be troublesome in times of shortage. Hence, elaborate measures were taken to ensure adequate supplies of grain and other necessities to the capital and large towns, and when goods were scarce maximum prices were often imposed.[52]

Of course, the rulers realized that a minimum of order and justice was necessary if the peasants were to produce the surplus on which they drew, and exhortations to apply both were frequent. But that seems to have been the sum total of interest in economic development. To quote Şerif Mardin:

> A shorthand notation for the Ottoman state may be "the fiscal state": by this is meant a state where major economic policy consisted in trying to maximize the tax yield from the rural economy. . . . But the attractiveness of grain culture [following the increased European demand for cereals] did not lead the Ottoman notables very far. The state had not engaged in the draining of marshes, the building of roads, the improvement of highways, the establishment of a postal system, and the dissemination of primary and secondary education as it had done in the West; it had not undergone a "mercantilist" phase of the Western European type; it did not have a "cameralist" phase with its economic engineering.[53]

Or, in Halil Inalcik's words: "The benefits of the state treasury and the needs of the internal market seem to be the only concerns of the Ottoman government."[54]

A few striking contrasts may be noted. Like Europe, but with a lag, the Ottoman Empire participated in the Price Revolution, and its currency suffered accordingly. But whereas the main European currencies were soon stabilized and experienced little or no depreciation thereafter, the Ottoman *akçe* showed a great, almost uninterrupted, decline beginning in the fifteenth century, well before the influx of American bullion, and continuing until the middle of the nineteenth century.[55] Stability was achieved in Europe not fortuitously but through the arduous efforts of the governments, as the history of Elizabeth's reign clearly shows, whereas in the Ottoman Empire (and Iran) the currency was continually debased. It should be added that, until the end of the seventeenth century, the power and resources of the Ottoman Empire were greater than those of any European country except perhaps Spain and France, which presumably implies that it had the means, but not the will or skill, to reform its currency.

We can also contrast attitudes to trade. Of course, the Middle Eastern rulers realized the importance of foreign trade, if only as a source of customs duties, and took some measures to stimulate it: for example, the building of caravanserais, upkeep of a few strategic roads, and privileges granted to European merchants.[56] But whereas the Europeans thought of trade as a means of increasing national wealth and employment, as well as holdings of bullion, and took what they thought to be appropriate measures, the Ottomans were concerned only with revenues and supplies; duties on exports were as high as those on imports and the exporting of certain goods was prohibited. This is often attributed to the Capitulations, and was no doubt perpetuated by them until the very eve of the First World War, in spite of the Ottoman desire to change the tariff.[57] The original policies, however, were adopted by the Ottomans at the height of their power, of their own free will. Clearly, these policies must either have been regarded as favorable to the interests of the empire or, if not, the economic consequences must have weighed little against the political advantages sought. Besides, as Halil Inalcik pointed out, in the sixteenth century the Capitulations were "very beneficial for the Ottoman economy" since they attracted trade.[58]

Indeed, I have not come across a single reference to such general concepts as "exports," "imports," and "balance of trade" in either Arabic or Turkish sources before the nineteenth century. I have asked several scholars who have worked in the Ottoman archives, both central and provincial, whether they had ever seen such concepts used, and have not yet had a positive answer. However, the argument from silence should not be pressed too far. Inalcik quotes a passage from Naima, written early in the eighteenth century, which states: "People in this country must abstain from the use of luxury goods of the countries hostile to the Ottoman empire and thus keep currency and goods from flowing out. They must use as much as possible the products of native industry."[59] And Berkes states: "It was also recognized that the financial well-being of the country depended upon a favorable balance of trade, and, as the main source of commerce was seaborne, it was believed necessary to create a Turkish merchant marine."[60] In practice, however, the government made no attempt to protect shipping by the kind of Navigation Acts prevalent in Europe.

One last point may be noted: the difference in the attitude toward industrialization in the Ottoman Empire and Europe. In the latter, because of the relatively greater economic and political power of the traders and craftsmen, there was much consideration for the interests of producers, often at the expense of consumers. In the Italian, German, Flemish, and Dutch city-states, traders and craftsmen were in fact the predominant power, and shaped economic policy to suit their interests. Again to quote Cipolla:

> In the majority of cases there was a conscious effort to industrialize. At the beginning of the fourteenth century the conviction was widespread that industry spelled welfare. In a Tuscan statute of 1336, statements may be read which might have been written by the most modern upholders of industrialization in the twentieth century.[61]

But even such national monarchies as England and France also took commercial and industrial needs into account. By the fourteenth century both England and France were enforcing measures designed to secure a favorable balance of trade by curtailing the import of competitive goods and encouraging that of inputs into goods that could supply local needs or be exported; by expanding exports, especially those with a large "value added" component, for example, cloth rather than raw wool; and, more generally, by stimulating local production. By the seventeenth century a full-fledged mercantilist theory had developed and, in the 1660s, Sir William Petty was expressing a very "modern" concern with production and employment as the basis of national prosperity. Such views had a marked effect on government policy.

In the Ottoman Empire, however, I have not come across anything other than a few attempts in the eighteenth century, mentioned by Mehmed Genç.[62]

What was the Ottoman legacy in economic thought and policy to the Arabs? First of all, there was the profound lack of interest in economic matters. This can be seen by looking at any history of Arab (or Turkish) thought, for example, the books by Albert Hourani, Raif Khuri, Niyazi Berkes, or Ahmet Sayar: the thinkers they studied were not interested in economics.

Starting in the 1830s, however, a certain concern with economic matters, and a realization of their importance, may be discerned in such Ottoman statesmen and thinkers as Sadik Rifaat, Sami, Cevdet, Mustafa Fazil (grandson of Mehmet Ali of Egypt), Khayr al-Din of Tunisia, and especially Namik Kemal, who during his stay in London imbibed Ricardian and Millsian principles. Their main emphasis was on the need for the state both to assure its subjects that they would enjoy the fruits of their labor and to remove various restrictions on their activity.

The translation of J. B. Say's *Catéchisme d'économie Politique* in 1852 and a book by Otto Hübner in 1869 constitute landmarks in modern Turkish thought. Say advocated Smithian liberalism and Hübner "national economy." Another landmark was the publication of Ahmed Midhat's *Ekonomi Politik* in 1286 (1869/70), which tried to take Ottoman conditions into account in expounding European principles of economics. Ohannes Effendi, who had studied in Paris and was to occupy many high posts, taught economics at the Mülkiye school and wrote a widely used textbook, *Mebadi-i Ilm-i servet-i Millel* (1297–1879/80). Another source of economic knowledge was the *Journal des Economistes*, to which many Ottomans subscribed. In 1911 Parvus (Alexander Helphand) came to Turkey, diffusing Marxist and antiimperialist ideas, and shortly after Tekin Alp (M. Cohen) wrote on economic matters in *Yeni Macmua*.[63]

Under the Young Turks, both before and during the First World War, many measures were taken to promote the economy and encourage the emergence of a national bourgeoisie, and many economic issues were debated. It was not, however, until the 1930s that the Turks had any adequately trained economists such as Ömer Celal Sarç. The same was true of the Arabs, with Muhammad Ali Rif'at and Nazmy Abd al-Hamid in Egypt or Sa'id Himadeh in Lebanon, or statisticians such as Hamed al-Azmy and R. al-Shannawany. The situation has, of course, greatly improved since then.

Second, there was a profound distrust of spontaneous economic activity and of market forces. It was almost axiomatic that if a man is making a profit he must be exploiting his workers, or the public, or both. Hence, the need for constant regulation of prices, wages, interest rates, and rent. This represents a Muslim tradition that goes back to the early Middle Ages.[64]

Third was the idea that the government should constantly be intervening in the economy, since it alone knows, and can implement, the public interest. Needless to say, this tendency has been greatly reinforced by European socialism and expressed itself in the wholesale, and on the whole disastrous, nationalizations of the 1960s in the Arab lands.

Last was a fiscalism that is only just being overcome—a preoccupation with government revenue, even at the cost of economic development.

In the fields of science, technology, and economics, the main Ottoman (and Mamluk) legacy in the Middle East was that, for over three centuries, the region was not prepared to learn from neighboring Europe. This meant that it did not enter the mainstream of progress in science and technology and it participated only marginally, and as a periphery, in Europe's economic activity and not at all in the development of its economic thought. In the last two hundred years the Middle East has made strenuous efforts to overcome the ensuing handicap, but it has done so under the unfavorable conditions resulting from European imperialism and the breakdown of the Ottoman Empire, and its success has been limited.

Three further observations are, however, necessary. First, it would be wrong to blame the Ottoman rulers for their indifference to science and economic activity, for that would be profoundly unhistorical. Like all peoples at all times, they had their priorities, which were not ours. Still, it would also be unreasonable to ignore the consequences of these priorities.

Second, if we accept the venerable (if historically inaccurate) European definition of the Ottomans as Turks and blend that in with the present-day (accurate) understanding of what is meant by Turk, then we can say that the Turks, rulers and subjects, did not exempt themselves from the burdens borne by the subject peoples. On the contrary, in addition to sharing in those ills, they suffered disproportionately from another one, the burden of military service, which fell heavily on them.

Third, during the last hundred years or so, the Turks (as defined above) have played a leading progressive role in the region. As Bernard Lewis has pointed out, much of the modern political thought of the Middle East (including Iran) originated in Ottoman official circles, and the Ottoman Turkish language was the route through which political concepts came to the Arabs. In the eighteenth century they had acquired a much fuller understanding of Western science and technology than their Asian fellow subjects—though not than their Greek and other Balkan ones.

But with the advent of Muhammad Ali, Egypt became the bellwether of the Middle East, the first country to lay down railways, build modern ports and irrigation works, send students to Europe, open Western-type schools, establish financial institutions, and achieve rapid economic growth. By the turn of the century, however, leadership passed back to Istanbul and has remained in the region that became Turkey. Many of the policies advocated by the Young Turks, especially the promotion of national as distinct from foreign enterprise and increasing state control over the economy, were emulated by the Arabs and Iranians, and most of Atatürk's reforms were imitated by both those peoples.

In many respects, the Arab countries and Iran followed, one generation behind, in the footsteps of Turkey. Thus, the policies of the 1950s and 1960s in the Arab lands recall those of Turkey in the 1920s and 1930s. One can only hope that Turkey's new political and economic trend will prove sufficiently successful to exert a similar effect on her Asian neighbors.[65]

Notes

1. For a fuller discussion, see Charles Issawi, "Reflections on the Study of Oriental Civilizations" in William Theodore de Bary and Ainslie Embree, *Approaches to Asian Civilization* (New York: Columbia University Press, 1964), reprinted in Charles Issawi, *The Arab Legacy* (Princeton: Darwin Press, 1981), pp. 147–56.

2. At the same time I am fully aware that religion is perhaps the most important single factor affecting the popular culture of a society, see Charles Issawi, "Empire Builders, Culture Makers, and Culture Imprinters," *Journal of Interdisciplinary History* 20, no. 2 (Autumn 1989):177–96.

3. See Charles Issawi, "The Middle East in the World Context," in Georges Sabagh, *The Modern Economic and Social History of the Middle East in Its World Context* (New York: Cambridge: Cambridge University Press, 1989), pp. 3–28.

4. See Charles Issawi, *An Economic History of the Middle East and North Africa* (New York: Columbia University Press, 1982).

5. See Ahmad Yusuf al-Hassan and Donald R. Hill, *Islamic Technology* (Cambridge: Cambridge University Press, 1986), pp. 16–17, 49, 59.

6. Edited and translated by Sevim Tekeli, *The Clocks in Ottoman Empire in 16th Century* (Ankara, 1966).

7. Abdulhak Adnan, *La Science chez les Turcs Ottomans* (Paris, 1939); Bernard Lewis, *The Muslim Discovery of Europe* (New York: Norton, 1982), pp. 227–28; Aydin Sayili, *The Observatory in Islam* (New York: Ayer, 1981).

8. I have been informed by Dr. Rushdi Rashed of the C.N.R.S. that certain eighteenth-century Egyptian manuscripts indicate an understanding of some aspects of European science, but to my knowledge no study has been made of these manuscripts.

9. UNESCO, *Statistical Yearbook 1989*, table 5.2.

10. E. Ashtor, *A Social and Economic History of the Near East in the Middle Ages* (Berkeley and Los Angeles: University of California Press, 1976), p. 50; O. G. Bolshakov, *Srednevekovyi Gorod Blizhnego Vostoka*, (Moscow, 1984), pp. 234–35.

11. B. H. Slicher van Bath, *Yield Ratios, 810–1820* (Wageningen, 1963) passim; Charles Issawi, *Economic History of Turkey* (Chicago: University of Chicago Press, 1980), pp. 214–25; Issawi, *The Fertile Crescent, 1800–1914* (New York: Oxford: Oxford University Press, 1988), p. 273; Issawi, *The Eco-*

nomic History of the Middle East (Chicago: University of Chicago Press, 1966), p. 377.

12. For the effects of Ottoman land laws in the Arab countries, see Gabriel Baer, "The Evolution of Private Landownership in Egypt and the Fertile Crescent," and Doreen Warriner, "Land Tenure in the Fertile Crescent," in Issawi, *Economic History of the Middle East*, pp. 71–90; Caglar Keyder and Faruk Tabak, *Landholding and Commercial Agriculture in the Middle East* (Albany: State University of New York Press, 1991).

13. Domenico Sella, "European Industries," in Carlo Cipolla, ed, *Fontana Economic History of Europe*, 2:395; John U. Nef in *Cambridge Economic History of Europe* (Cambridge: Cambridge University Press, 1952), 2:458–69; H. Kellenbenz, *Cambridge Economic History*, 4:472–75.

14. B. Lewis, *Muslim Discovery of Europe*, p. 225.

15. Thomas Thornton, *The Present State of Turkey* (London, 1807), p. 24.

16. See Issawi, *Economic History of Turkey*, p. 284. For other equally unfavorable opinions, see pp. 281–88.

17. B. Lewis, *Muslim Discovery of Europe*, pp. 225–26.

18. V. Parry, "La Manière de combattre," in V. Parry and M. E. Yapp, *War, Technology, and Society in the Middle East* (New York: Oxford: Oxford University Press, 1975), p. 246.

19. See Charles Issawi, "Population and Resources," in Thomas Naff and Roger Owen, eds., *Studies in Eighteenth-Century Islamic History* (Carbondale: Southern Illinois University Press, 1977), pp. 160–61.

20. Dispatch from Carmarthen, March 15, 1789, PRO FO 78/10.

21. E. Ashtor, "L'apogée du commerce vénitien," *Venezia centro di Mediazione*, vol. 1 (Florence, 1977), pp. 318–21.

22. For details, see Issawi, *The Arab Legacy*, pp. 93–96; Issawi, *An Economic History of the Middle East and North Africa*, pp. 150–54, and sources cited.

23. See Issawi, *Economic History of Turkey*, pp. 314–15; Johannes Pederson, *The Arabic Book* (Princeton: Princeton University Press, 1984), pp. 60–67. For the Byzantines, see N. G. Wilson, *Scholars of Byzantium* (Baltimore: Johns Hopkins University Press, 1983), pp. 63–65.

24. Pederson, pp. 132–37; Şerif Mardin, "Some Notes on an Early Phase in the Modernization of Turkey," *Comparative Studies in Society and History* 3:3 (April 1961).

25. See Charles Issawi, "Technology, Energy, and Civilization," *IJMES* (August 1991) and Jean Gimpel, *The Medieval Machine* (New York: Penguin, 1976).

26. Ashtor, *Social and Economic History*, p. 308; Abd al-Rahman al-Jabarti, *'ajaib al athar*, vol 2 (Beirut, 1978), p. 231; S. Avitsur, "Wind Power in the Technological Development of Palestine," in David Kushner, ed., *Palestine in the Late Ottoman Period* (Jerusalem-Leiden: E. J. Brill, 1986), pp. 231–44; in the tenth century, al-Mas'udi discussed windmills, see Max

Meyerhoff, "Science and Medicine" in Sir Thomas Arnold and Alfred Guillaume, eds., *The Legacy of Islam* (London, 1931), p. 333.

27. In this section I have drawn on my "Europe, the Middle East, and the Shift in Power," *Arab Legacy*, pp. 111–31.

28. See A. L. Udovitch, *Partnership and Profit in Medieval Islam*, (Princeton: Princeton University Press, 1970); Halil Inalcik, "Capital Formation in the Ottoman Empire," *Journal of Economic History* 29:1 (March 1969).

29. For examples, see Inalcik, "Capital Formation in the Ottoman Empire."

30. See sources cited in Issawi, *Economic History of the Middle East and North Africa*, p. 260n10 and Issawi, *Fertile Crescent*, pp. 443–45; also Inalcik, "Capital Formation in the Ottoman Empire."

31. Geoffrey Parker, "The Emergence of Modern Finance," in Carlo Cipolla, *Fontana Economic History*, 2:443–45.

32. Issawi, *Economic History of Turkey*, pp. 339–41, 321.

35. R. De Roover, "The Organization of Trade"; M. M. Postan et al., *Cambridge Economic History of Europe*, 3:99–100 and *Encyclopaedia Britannica*, 11th ed. s.v. "Insurance."

34. Issawi, *Economic History of Turkey*, p. 326; Issawi, *Fertile Crescent*, p. 412; for the late Ottoman view of insurance see Niyazi Berkes, *The Development of Secularism in Turkey* (Montreal: McGill University Press, 1964), pp. 398–99.

35. For an excellent survey, see Joseph Schumpeter, *History of Economic Analysis* (New York: Oxford University Press, 1954).

36. For an illuminating example, see Issawi, *Arab Legacy*, pp. 119–20.

37. Schumpeter, *History of Economic Analysis*, p. 14.

38. Ibid., pp. 13–14, 526.

39. See M. A. Nashaat, "Ibn Khaldun, Pioneer Economist," *Egypte Contemporaine* 38 (1944); Charles Issawi, *An Arab Philosophy of History* (London, 1950), introduction, chs. 3 and 4.

40. Cemal Kafadar, "When Coins Turned Into Drops of Dew and Bankers Became Robbers of Shadows: The Boundaries of Ottoman Economic Imagination at the End of the Sixteenth Century," Ph.D. dissertation, McGill University, October 1986; see also Ahmed Sayat, *Osmanli Iktisat Düsüncesinin Cagdas Casması* (Istanbul, 1986).

41. Kafadar, pp. 108–9. All Ottoman statesmen and writers took for granted that economic forces and activities should be firmly under the control of the political authorities. In fairness to them, it should be pointed out that for a long time this system worked, i.e., the economy was able to produce the surplus revenue required for administration, war, and the luxury consumption of the rulers. Indeed in the sixteenth century, except for technological innovation, the Ottoman Empire did not compare unfavorably with Europe—see Charles Issawi's "The Ottoman-Hapsburg Balance of Forces" in Halil Inalcik and Cemal Kafadar, *Empire and Civilization in the Age of Suleyman* (Istanbul, 1991). It was only very slowly, with the sustained rise

of Europe and decline of the Ottoman Empire, that the inadequacy of the economy became apparent, causing an eventual opening up in the nineteenth century. This presents a striking analogy with the Soviet Union, whose economy "worked" for a long time, producing a large surplus for investment and defense, but eventually was unable to keep up with the West.

42. Cornell H. Fleischer, *Bureaucrat and Intellectual in the Ottoman Empire: The Historian Mustafa Ali (1541–1600)* (Princeton: Princeton University Press, 1986), pp. 4, 8. 235.

43. Andreas Tietze, *Mustafa Ali's Counsel for Sultans Edition, Translation, Notes*, 2 vols. (Vienna: Verlag der Oesterreichen Akademie der Wissenschaften, 1979, 1982).

44. For the latter see Schumpeter, *History of Economic Analysis*, and Eric Roll, *A History of Economic Thought* (London, n.d.), ch. 2.

45. *Mustafa Ali's Counsel*, vol. 1, pp. 19, 39, 57, 59–62, 65, 66, 71, 82; vol. 2, pp. 11, 26, 30, 34.

46. Andreas Tietze, *Mustafa Ali's Description of Cairo of 1599* (Vienna: Verlag der Oesterreichischen Akademie der Wissenschaften, 1975).

47. See B. Lewis, "Ottoman Observers of Ottoman Decline," *Islam in History* (New York, 1973), pp. 199–213; Issawi, *Arab Legacy*, pp. 117–22.

48. An important exception, pointed out to me by Mr. Rabah Shahbandar, is the Nilometer of Egypt, which goes back to antiquity. The height of the Nile is often mentioned by historians. Presumably, knowing the exact height of the Nile on which crops—and therefore taxes—depended was too important a matter to be left to approximation.

49. Inalcik and Kafadar, *Empire and Civilization in the Age of Suleyman*, pp. 58–59.

50. See Issawi, "Population and Resources," *Economic History of Turkey*, pp. 389.

51. Quoted in the *Cambridge Economic History of Europe*, 3:281.

52. For eighteenth- and early nineteenth-century Istanbul, see Issawi, *Economic History of Turkey*, pp. 24–33, which includes a translation of an article by Lütfi Gücer on grain supply; see also the very informative article by W. Hahn, "Die Verpflegung Konstantinopels durch staatliche Zwangswirtschaft," *Beihefte zur Vierteljahrschrift für Sozial und Wirtschaftsgeschichte* 7 (1926). For the 16th century, Rhoades Murphey, "Provisioning Istanbul: The State and Subsistence in the Early Middle East," *Food and Foodways*, vol 2 (London, 1988).

53. Şerif Mardin, "The Transformation of an Economic Code," in Ergun Ozbudun and Aydin Ulusan, eds., *The Political Economy of Income Distribution in Turkey* (New York: Holmes and Meier, 1980), p. 29.

54. Halil Inalcik, "The Ottoman Economic Mind," in Michael Cook, ed., *Studies in the Economic History of the Middle East* (New York: Oxford: Oxford University Press, 1970), p. 212.

55. See graph in *Cambridge Economic History of Europe*, 4:458; O. L. Barkan, "The Price Revolution of the Sixteenth Century," *IJMES*, 1975;

Issawi, *The Economic History of Turkey*, ch. 7. For an excellent and analytic account of the debasement of the Ottoman currency, see Inalcik and Kafadar, *Empire and Civilization in the Age of Suleyman*, ch. 1; it is worth noting that the late-sixteenth-century historian Selaniki contrasted unfavorably Ottoman monetary policy with that of contemporary Europe (pp. 100–101).

56. Halil Inalcik, *The Ottoman Empire in the Classical Age* (London: Caratzas, 1973), pp. 121–66; Inalcik, "Capital Formation in the Ottoman Empire"; Carl M. Kortepeter, "Ottoman Imperial Policy and the Economy of the Black Sea Region in the Sixteenth Century," *Journal of the American Oriental Society* 86, no. 2 (April–June 1966).

57. Issawi, *The Economic History of Turkey*, ch. 3.

58. Inalcik, "The Ottoman Economic Mind," pp. 214–15.

59. Ibid., p. 215.

60. Berkes, *Development of Secularism in Turkey*, p. 74.

61. *Cambridge Economic History of Europe*, 3:413 and, more generally, pp. 408–19.

62. *La Révolution industrielle dans le Sud-Est européen* (Sofia, 1976).

63. See Şerif Mardin, *The Genesis of Young Ottoman Thought* (Princeton: Princeton University Press, 1962); Mardin, "Türkiyede Iktisadi Düsüncenin Gelismesi" (Ankara, 1962); and Ahmet Sayar, *Osmanli iktisat*. I am indebted to Nilüfer Hatimi, a graduate student at Princeton, for help in reading these books.

64. See Inalcik, "Capital Formation." The opinion of Jurji Zaydan may also be quoted: "Trade is the most important source of income in our country. Yet is part of the popular phantasies that wealth is not (to be) attained in a legitimate, *halal* manner," Thomas Philipp, *Gurgi Zaydan* (Beirut 1979), pp. 14–15.

65. Since this chapter was written two important articles have appeared: Cemal Kafadar, "Les troubles monetaires de la fin du XVIe siecle et la prise de conscience ottomane du declin," *Annales, ESC* (March–April 1991), an excellent account of the Ottoman price inflation that develops further some of the points made in his thesis (see note 40); and Virginia H. Aksan, "Ottoman Political Writing, 1768–1808," *International Journal of Middle East Studies* 25:1 (February 1993):55–69, which has valuable information, particularly regarding the views of Ahmed Resmi and Koca Sekbanbasi on military reform. Neither article, however, requires modification of the general interpretation presented here.

SIX

THE GREEKS IN THE
MIDDLE EAST

The Ottoman Empire was ruled by Turks and other Ottoman-ized Muslims, including the Janissaries. Muslims commanded the armies and constituted the bulk of land forces. They governed the provinces (*eyalet* or *pashaliks*) and dispensed justice in the *qadi* courts. They formed the overwhelming majority of the *timariots* and *zaims*, who, in return for assignments of land, administered the countryside, raised taxes, and provided military service. They staffed the bureaucracy and controlled and dispensed Muslim education. Lastly, and most important, it was from their ranks that the sultan chose his advisers and ministers. In short, in more ways than one, the Ottoman Empire was what the Greeks called it—a *Tourkokratia*.

Rulers often have neither the aptitude nor the inclination to pursue other activities besides government, however, and, like others before them, the Turks delegated many economic, social, and cultural activities to their *millets*: the Orthodox, including the Greeks, the Armenians, the Jews, and those of other minorities.

The role of the Greeks in the empire shows a clear trend: a slow rise followed by a somewhat swifter decline. Whereas, at all times, the Greeks were the most numerous non-Muslim millet in the empire, in the second half of the fifteenth and during the early sixteenth century, the Jewish millet was the most prominent, though the part played by Bosnians and Serbs should not be underestimated. Tens of thousands of Jews immigrated from the Iberian Peninsula and Italy to Constantinople, Thessaloniki, Smyrna, Adrianople, and elsewhere, and many were relocated by the sultan to other parts of the empire. Many of these immigrants possessed valuable skills that enabled them to achieve a measure of success. For example, European-trained Jewish physicians rose to positions of distinction; some even served as personal physicians to the sultans. Jewish print-ers set up the first presses in the empire and, starting in 1494, pro-duced texts in European languages as well as in Hebrew but not in Arabic or Turkish, as the printing of texts in these languages was prohibited by Bayezid II in 1485.[1]

Since these immigrants knew European languages, and the sul-tans often regarded them as more trustworthy than Christians, they were sent abroad on diplomatic and other missions. Many Jews also set up banks and shops and at times controlled the customshouses and the mint, and, as they often had good foreign contacts, they played a leading role in foreign trade. The appointment of Joseph Nasi as "Duke of Naxos," with the rank of *sancak beyi*, marks the apogee of Jewish influence.[2] Jewish influence declined sharply in later years. One reason was possibly Sabbatai Sevi's (1626–1676) messianic claims, which prompted many Jews to sever their contacts with European learning and technology. Another was the increas-ingly strict enforcement of the empire's policy of Muslim control over *dhimmis*. In addition, other Europeans, protected by the Capitu-lations, were gaining influence in certain economic sectors and thus had developed a bourgeoisie well before the Ottoman communities.

The vacuum left by the Jews was, in due course, filled mostly by the Greeks, the most active group within the Orthodox millet. A number of factors can account for this. The Greeks were a highly urbanized community. They formed a large proportion of the popu-lation of the biggest and most active towns, notably Constanti-nople, Smyrna, and Thessaloniki. Their position on either side of the Aegean put them athwart the busy trade route connecting Con-stantinople and the Black Sea with the Mediterranean and Europe. Because of the paucity of natural resources in mainland Greece, Greeks had become over the years deeply engaged in commerce and shipping and thus had developed a bourgeoisie well before other communities. In addition, the empire prohibited Europeans from do-ing business in the Black Sea area. Most of the merchants in the Black Sea area were Muslims, but the Greeks soon gained a promi-nent role in that trade, especially in the wheat supply of Constan-tinople. When Russia began trading through the Black Sea, more-over, it was largely in Greek ships, sailing under the Russian flag, and through Greek merchant houses.[3] The large Greek diaspora, first in Italy and the Balkans, then in Russia, Egypt, central and western Europe, and, finally, in the Americas, also provided this community with a flow of ideas, funds, and various other kinds of support that helped their kin in the empire.

Together with the Armenians, Greeks were far more educated than other communities. From the sixteenth century on, graduates of the Greek College in Rome and the schools set up by Greeks in Venice returned home, bringing with them elements of European culture and Greek books published in Venice and elsewhere—an estimated 2,500 titles between about 1750 and 1821.[4] This was followed by the founding of Greek schools and the setting up of printing presses in Constantinople and elsewhere.[5] Greeks also had contacts with the Western world through the Venetians (and later French, Russians, and British), who controlled the Ionian islands.[6] The Patriarchal Academy, founded in 1454 in Constantinople, was also an important resource for the Greeks of the empire. It trained the Phanariots (rich Greek merchants of that city who played a leading part in the church), staffed the upper ranks of the Foreign Ministry (Dragoman to the Sublime Porte), provided the governors (*hospodars*) of Moldavia and Wallachia, and supplied influential interpreters (dragomans) to foreign embassies.[7]

The international prominence of the Greek language also was a significant factor in the rise of the Greek millet. The Greek language provided a link with Byzantium (and later in the form of archaizing *katharevousa* with classical Hellas), giving the Greeks a prestige and inspiration unavailable to any other millet. It also provided them with a more immediate advantage. "Thousands of Albanians and Vlachs became Hellenized through their membership in the Greek Orthodox Church," including the many Albanians who migrated to Greece in the seventeenth and eighteenth centuries.[8] In addition, "Greek was the commerical *lingua franca* of much of the Balkan mercantile bourgeoisie."[9]

Greek influence in the Ottoman Empire probably reached its peak in the fist decades of the nineteenth century, just before the War of Independence. The war and its aftermath led to a sharp decline in the Greek population. First of all, the new Hellenic state accounted for perhaps 800,000 Greeks, or about a quarter of the estimated number of Greeks in the empire. This proportion rose steadily thanks to both a high birth rate and reunification. These more than offset emigration from Greece to the Ottoman Empire and elsewhere. By 1907, the population of independent Greece was 2.6 million, a figure that exceeded that of the Greeks in the empire (about 2 million).[10] Second, the war inflicted large losses of lives and property on the Greeks, as well as on the Turks. Third, the Porte was severely shaken by the Greek revolt and never again permitted its Greek subjects to exercise the kind of power they had once enjoyed.

The Greeks' loss of power coincided with, and was facilitated by, the rise of the Armenians, who had considerable influence until the end of the nineteenth century. Like the Greeks, they had also established contacts with Europe, sent young men to be trained in Italy and elsewhere, set up printing presses, promoted education, and profited greatly from their diaspora, which gave them contacts not only with Europe and Russia but also with Iran and India.[11] It appears, moreover, that Armenians spoke Turkish at home more often than did Greeks. This may have helped them in their dealings with Turks and enabled them to play a more ctive role in the cultural affairs of the empire.

The part played by Greeks and Armenians, and to a lesser extent by Jews, in the economic life of the empire was enormous.[12] In certain fields, this was already apparent at the beginning of the nineteenth century. For example, the overwhelming majority of *sarrafs* (moneylenders who also often acted as tax farmers) were members of these groups, trade between the Balkans and Austria was largely in Greek hands, and Greeks played a part in Ottoman sea trade with Europe.[13] In industry and various branches of trade, the influence of the millets increased steadily up to the First World War. Starting at the top, with bankers and bank managers, Table 6.1 shows the situation in 1912.

TABLE 6.1.

Place	Total of bankers	Greeks	Armenians	Jews	Turks	Other and unidentified
Constantinople	40	12	12	8	0	8
European provinces	32	22	3	3	0	4
Anatolia	90	40	27	0	2	21
	162	74	42	11	2	32

SOURCE: P. Marouche and G. Sarantis, *Annuaire Financier de la Turquie* (Pera: 1912), pp. 137–40.

We should add that Greeks continued to be influential at both ends of the scale. On the one hand, some of the Galata bankers, such as the bankers Zariphis and Zographos, worked directly with sultans Abdul-Hamid and Murad, for example. And, on the other hand, many remained active as moneylenders and tax farmers in the villages.

The situation in industry was similar, but here one cannot be so precise, since many establishments, especially the larger ones, were listed under the name of the firm, not that of the owner. A perusal of the 1913 census returns shows that Turkish Muslims appear much more frequently here than in finance, but still constitute a small minority. In the silk industry, Armenian names prevail and, in the cigarette-paper industry, Jewish. In other branches of industry, the predominance of Greeks is very clear.[14] A study by the Turkish scholar Tevfik Çavdar puts the distribution of 284 industrial firms employing five or more workers as follows: Greek, 50 percent; Armenians, 20; Turks, 15; Jews, 5; and foreigners, 10. Their labor force was 60 percent Greek; 15 percent Armenian; 15 percent Turkish; and 10 percent Jewish.[15] A breakdown of firms in industry and crafts in 1912 (6,507) shows that 49 percent were Greek; 30 Armenian; 12 Turkish; and 10 other.[16]

The predominance of the millets in the industrial labor force was reinforced by the fact that their women, unlike Turkish women, worked in factories. In Bursa in 1872, only 4 percent of workers in silk-reeling plants were men. These men were foremen, engine drivers, and packers. The rest of the work force was made up of women and girls, 95 percent of whom were Greek or Armenian. "The authorities endeavor to discourage and prevent the employment of Turkish women in factories," a report from the period advises. Turkish women sometimes found the wages tempting and later did join the labor force in increasing numbers.[17] Workers from the millets formed a large proportion of the skilled labor force and also played a leading role in organizing workers in large enterprises in Constantinople, Smyrna, and Thessaloniki. They played leading roles in the strikes that broke out in these cities after the promulgation of the 1908 Constitution.[18]

In the nineteenth century, Greeks became prominent in foreign trade. In the 1830s, Greeks opened offices in England. By the 1850s, they had 55 firms in Manchester and 14 in London; by 1870, there were 167 Greek firms in Manchester.[19] These firms were probably engaged in exporting textiles, and some remained prominent until the outbreak of the Second World War. A list of the large importers of textiles in Constantinople in 1906 shows 26 Armenian names, 5 Turkish, 3 Greek, and 1 Jewish. In 1910, of 28 large firms in Constantinople importing Russian goods, 5 were Russian, 8 Muslim, 7 Greek, 6 Armenian, and 2 were Jewish; almost all large traders with Russia in the eastern provinces were Armenians.[20] In 1912, of 18,063 firms engaged in internal trade, 43 percent were Greek, 23 Armenian, 15 Muslim, and 19 other.[21] Of the membership of the Chamber of Commerce of Constantinople, Turks and foreigners each formed about 25 percent, "the balance, often exceeding 50 percent of the total," was composed of members from the Greek, Armenian, and Jewish minorities.[22] In Smyrna, at the turn of this century, as Elena Frangakis-Syrett has shown, "Greek merchants made up between 40 and 50 percent of the city's merchants, Ottomans and Westerners included," and were particularly prominent in the cloth, wine, and liquor trade, as well as in that of the main export items, such as figs, raisins, and olive oil. In addition, as early as 1896, the Greeks of Samsun controlled 156 businesses out of a total of 214.[23] Lastly, in Trebizond, in 1884, of 110 merchants listed as engaged in foreign trade as commission agents, exporters, and importers (there was some overlap in these categories), 48 had recognizably Greek names and 40 Armenian.[24]

As I have said, Greeks of course also played an important part in navigation, particularly in coastal shipping. During much of the nineteenth century, many Greek ships sailed under either Ottoman or Hellenic flags. For example, in 1850 Rhodes and its three tiny neighbors (Cassos, Castel Rosso, and Symi) had 142 locally built vessels aggregating 27,000 tons under Ottoman flag and 54 aggregating 12,000 under Greek.[25] The growth of steam navigation in the eastern Mediterranean adversely affected Greek sailing ships, however, and several islands lost much of their population. "The crisis was overcome when wealthy overseas Greeks began to purchase old steamships in England and to lease them to captains in Greece" and, we may presume, to Ottoman Greeks. "Large profits were made during the South Africa War, and the capital was used to buy still more steamships." By 1915, there were 475 steamers, aggregating 894,000 tons, under the Greek flag alone.[26] Several Greek or Ottoman Greek lines were actively engaged in the trade of İzmir (e.g., Papayani Brothers, Pantaleon Oriental Navigation Co., etc.) according to Frangakis-Syrett. As early as 1842, Greek flag steamers were also plying along the Black Sea coast as far as Samsun, and, in 1896, two out of 10 steamship lines calling at Trebizond were Greek.[27] In fiscal 1912 to 1913, over 10 percent of the shipping calling at Constantinople was under Greek flag. Presumably, a large part of the 11 percent under Ottoman flag was Greek-owned.[28] Needless to say, the Greek lines employed Ottoman Greeks as agents, as did certain other lines.[29]

Greeks were also well-represented in the professions up to the First World War. In 1912, Greeks accounted for 52 percent of physicians (Armenians 17, Turks 10); 52 percent of architects (34 and 5); 49 percent of pharmacists (25 and 11); 37 percent of engineers (11 and 2); and 29 percent of lawyers (21 and 38).[30]

Within the government bureaucracy, after 1821 Greeks never recovered the influence that the Phanariots had enjoyed before that date. They were, however, well-represented in those branches where their skills were needed, notably the ministries of Foreign Affairs and Agriculture. I suspect that many Greeks served in the Public Debt Administration, but have not been able to locate any evidence.[31]

Largely due to the excellent studies by Carter V. Findley, abundant material is available on the ethnic composition of the Foreign Ministry and on the education and career patterns of its officials. In the sample he studied, the share of Greeks rose from 4 percent in 1850 to a peak of 10 in 1882, declining to 7 by 1908, as the number of qualified Turks increased. The Greek component was consistently smaller than that of the Armenians (11, 18, and 13), but much higher than that of the Jews.[32] Here, too, a key reason for the better showing of the Armenians was likely to have been their greater knowledge of Turkish: 85 percent of Armenians claimed proficiency in Turkish as compared to 77 percent of Greeks. Conversely, Greeks seem to have endeavored to master European languages, most significantly French.[33] Another factor is of course the clannishness of minorities and their tendency to appoint, support, and promote their own members. Thus, Armenians were heavily concentrated in the Foreign Correspondence Office and Office of Legal Council, which had been headed at an early stage by prominent Armenians.[34] Greeks, however, were prominent in the diplomatic, consular, and commercial departments. For illustration we can mention John Aristarchis, who served for a long period as ambassador to Berlin; or Constantine Mousouros, Constantine Anthopoulos, and Stephen Mousouros who, among them, headed the embassy in London from 1856 to 1901. Most surprising, Stephen Mousouros became ambassador to Greece itself. Alexander Karatheodoris was ambassador in Rome and a leading Ottoman delegate at the Congress of Berlin; he rose twice to ministerial rank, serving, at different times, as minister of foreign affairs and minister of public works. There was also a Greek member in all the Young Turk cabinets, from 1908 to 1912, usually in one of the more technical ministries such as Mines, Forestry, or Agriculture.[35]

In the Ministry of Agriculture, however, Armenians seem to have played a much more prominent part than Greeks. In the 1870s, two Armenian agriculture directors were appointed and soon after were joined by other officials. A list of agricultural inspectors serving in Anatolia in the period from 1883 to 1908 shows four Armenian names as against two Greek and six Turkish, with two uncertain.[36]

The high position occupied by Greeks (and Armenians) in business, the professions, and government service was due to their advanced educational level. Findley's breakdown of Foreign Ministry officials shows that some 63 percent of Muslims obtained their elementary schooling in Quranic schools, where they received poor training. The schools attended by minorities were distinctly better. The same discrepancy held at all subsequent levels and was particularly marked at the higher ones. Table 6.2 gives a breakdown of Foreign Ministry officials.

As in the past, Ottoman Greeks continued to go abroad for a university education, including the kingdom of Greece. In addition, from the middle of the nineteenth century, efforts were made to expand and improve Greek schools within the empire. By the 1870s, there were 105 schools in Constantinople, including 22 girls' schools, with 15,000 pupils, entirely supported by private funds.[37] By 1920, the Greater Constantinople area had over 30,000 pupils—some 10

TABLE 6.2. Percentage of Officials in Sample

	Muslims	Greeks	Armenians
Studied in higher and professional schools	50	77	50
Completed higher education	20	50	19
Studied at university	4	27	14
Received university degree	2	10	10

SOURCE: C. Findley, *Ottoman Civil Officialdom* (Princeton: Princeton University Press, 1989), Table 4.7, p. 162.

percent of the total Greek population.[38] In these schools Greek children learned foreign languages (mainly French) and business skills that enabled them to compete successfully with other groups.

So far I have focused on Greeks living in urban areas, but 70 to 75 percent of all Ottoman Greeks lived in the countryside.[39] The situation of these Greeks was very different. The bulk of the agricultural land belonged to Muslims, and large properties were, with few exceptions, in Muslim hands.[40] Most of the land was (and still is) planted with cereals and farmed by Muslims. In the farming of cash crops, however, the millets played an important part. In the words of an acute observer: "Their [Greeks and Armenians] broader [*ganzer*] mind, which is more oriented toward gain, leads them in mass to the cultivation of cash crops and also fruits. Thus they frequently prefer the cultivation of vegetables, tobacco, mulberries, and other fruit to that of cereals because the former present greater prospect of gain [of course that does not prevent the Greeks or the Armenians from stepping in after the harvest, buying the Turkish peasants' crops, and conveying them to the towns—footnote in original]. And through this greater sense of profit they usually push out of agriculture those Turks whom they find in their way." In fruits and cash crops the leading role in western Asia Minor was played by Greeks, further east by Armenians, and to a small extent in Palestine by Jews. In the growing of mulberries (for silkworm breeding) the leading groups in western Asia Minor were the Armenians and the Greeks, in Syria the Christian Arabs.[41] It may be added that in the most rapidly expanding sector of agriculture, cotton, the main thrust came from Greeks. In the Smyrna region, cotton farms belonged "mostly to Greeks, but also to Turks," whereas in Adana, of the large landowners using modern methods, "few are pure Turks, but rather Greeks, Armenians, Syrians and so on."[42] Greek predominance was even more apparent in spinning and weaving, and cottonseed oil pressing in Adana, the development of which must have had a stimulative effect on cotton growing.

The progress of Greeks and Armenians in agriculture was helped by their greater access to justice after the Tanzimat reforms and their ability to take advantage of the introduction of Western concepts of land property. Another great advantage was their exclusion from the army. Consider three examples. In Erzurum, in 1848: "The Armenians have more hands, the Mussulman youth being taken for military service. The Mussulmans do not hire labor and they are unable to cultivate the extent of land they possess." In Biga in 1860: "Their

[Christians'] pecuniary means being larger than those of the Mussulmans, they are constantly purchasing property from the latter"; in the past this had been prohibited. In Smyrna, at the same time, "The Christian races are buying up the Turks; the Turks, handicapped by conscription, fall into the hands of some Christian usurious banker (Armenian, Greek, or occasionally European) to whom the whole property or estate is soon sacrificed."[43] As a British diplomat observed: "But when force does not rule, when progress, commerce, finance and law give the mixed population of the Empire a chance of redistributing themselves according to their wits, the Turk and the Christian are not equal; the Christian is superior. He acquires the money and land of the Turk, and proves in a lawcourt that he is right in so doing."[44] The advance of the Greeks into western Anatolia was noted by many observers. "Everyone who has any familiarity with the Aeolic and Ionian coasts knows of many a flourishing Greek village, which not so many years ago was empty or peopled only by Turks. The Turks are losing, or have in places lost, their hold on the coast and on the valleys that open on the coast. . . . As the railway goes inland, the Greek element goes with it and even in front of it."[45]

This feeling of being overwhelmed and driven out of the countryside caused much resentment among Turks and helps to account for the intense bitterness and violence in the struggle among Turks, Armenians, and Greeks in the period from 1895 to 1923.[46]

Nowhere else in the Middle East, except in Egypt, did the Greeks occupy a position commensurate with the one they had in Turkey. Unlike other minorities (Copts, Syrians, Armenians, and Jews), the Greeks in Egypt were never in a position to influence Egyptian politics or contribute to Arab culture, though they did produce a large number of minor scientists as well as prominent physicians, engineers, and lawyers in the Mixed Courts, where the language was French. They can also boast of modern Alexandria's most distinguished son, the poet Constantin Cavafy. In the economy, they operated at every layer, from large-scale banking and cotton exporting (Salvago, Benaki, and others) through internal trade to village grocery stores. They played a leading part in the development of long staple cotton, commemorated by such varieties as Sakellarides, Zagora, Yannovitch, Pilion, and others and reintroduced vine growing (Gianaclis). They were prominent in cotton ginning, cigarette manufacturing, and other industries and played an active part in construction work, hotels, and Nile transport. Lastly they were well represented among the employees and skilled workers not only of Greek but of other firms.[47]

The Greeks played a similar, though distinctly smaller, role in the Sudan. They first penetrated the country in the middle of the nineteenth century, during the Egyptian occupation, and reentered literally on the heels of the British army of reconquest, to Lord Cromer's amazement and slight amusement.[48] However, they were less prominent in the upper layers, though they did have some leading merchants and contractors such as Kondomikhalos.

In Iran, the main Greek interest consisted of firms established in Tabriz conducting trade through Trebizond, the main outlet for Iran's foreign trade.[49] Of these, the main one was the Ralli and Agelasto firm, connected with the well known Ralli Brothers, which had been established in London in 1818 and had branches in Marseilles, Odessa, and Constantinople and, by the 1850s, in India. The owner of the Tabriz firm was a Russian national who later became a British subject. There was also another Greek firm in Tabriz. At the Trebizond and Constantinople ends, all non-Persian firms trading with Iran seem to have been Greek.[50] Ralli and other Greek firms also played an important part in the silk trade of Gilan, advancing funds to growers, buying their crops, and, when the muscardine blight struck in 1864, introducing disease-resistant eggs, first from Japan and later from Bursa.[51]

In Iraq, Greek firms played a minor role in foreign trade. We know of two in Baghdad in 1857 and two in Basra in 1891.[52] I am confident that research will reveal the presence of Greek merchants and shipping agents in various parts of the Arabian Peninsula. In Syria, however, I have not come across any signs of Greek trading activity. A few Greeks settled along the coast, such as the Katzeflis, Katafago, and Avierinos families, but they intermarried with local Christians and most were soon assimilated. The only Greek economic activity I have come across was sponge fishing. In 1839, it was reported that some 300 divers from the Castel Rosso archipelago came to Tripoli each year and fished for sponges; by 1912, their number had fallen to 80, the divers having migrated to the United States.[53] Of course, there was also much Greek shipping calling at the Syrian ports. In 1899, for example, 55 ships, aggregating 15,000 tons, entered Beirut under the Greek flag, and a substantial proportion of the 2,739 vessels (143,000 tons) carrying the Ottoman flag must also have been Greek-owned.[54]

Mention should also be made of the role of the higher Greek clergy in the Syrian Orthodox Patriarchate, a matter that attracted much attention and controversy at the end of the nineteenth century.

So far, I have dwelt on Greeks in the economic life of the empire. This is partly because I am most familiar with this aspect of Greek history during this period, partly because it lends itself, more than others, to quantitative analysis. I will conclude with some discussion of the culture and politics of the region during this period.

First of all, a distinction must be made between the cultural advance of Ottoman Greeks and their influence on Turkish cultural development. On the first matter, in addition to the schools mentioned earlier, there were the *syllogoi* (cultural associations), of which there were 26 in Constantinople alone in the early 1870s, and more later.[55] In addition to their educational, literary, and social work, these associations were active in disseminating Hellenic ideals. They were supported exclusively by private funds.

The Greek contribution to the development of Turkish culture, though considerable, seems to have fallen short of that of the Armenians. Here, again, one gets the impression that, through language, the Armenians were closer to the Turks and therefore could more easily pioneer and participate in such activities as the theater, journalism, and music.[56] Prominent among Greek contributions were translations from European languages, even after their monopoly as dragomans was broken following the Greek revolt in 1821; here again one may mention Alexander Karatheodoris. In journalism, in the 1870s, Theodore Kassape edited *Diojen*, which published some of Namik Kemal's articles; he also edited the satirical journal *Hayal* in which he published a translation of Molière's *L'Avare*. One may also mention Alexander Istamatyadi, who wrote a patriotic play, *Gazi Osman* (1878).[57] Of course, Greeks exercised a much wider, though much more difficult to trace, influence through such aspects of social life as dress, manners, and lifestyle.

For politics, it is tempting, but ultimately misleading to think of the Ottoman Greeks purely in terms of modern nationalism and the desire for unification with the Kingdom of Greece. Two essays[58] show the complexity of the issues. One by Paraskevas Konortas points to the dangers of identifying Orthodoxy with Hellenism or the Roman (*Rumi*) religious community with the Greek nation. The changes in the title of the ecumenical patriarch of Constantinople between the sixteenth and nineteenth centuries show both the complexity of the evolution of relations between Greeks and other Orthodox Ottomans and the shifts in the attitude of Ottoman authorities towards these relations. An essay by Richard Clogg[59] explores a fundamental fact of Middle Eastern politics, the primacy of religion. The Turkish-speaking Karamanlı Christians of Anatolia wrote in the Greek alphabet but do not seem to have considered themselves Greeks. They conducted at least part of their liturgy in Greek, but otherwise used Turkish. Efforts were made by various Greek societies, in both the kingdom and the empire, to re-Hellenize the Karamanlıs, by sending them teachers and books and educating their young men in Athens, but they "met with mixed success," and the increasing number of translations into Karamanlı Turkish from both European languages and Greek shows that the Karamanlıs continued to cling to their tongue. Not surprisingly, in 1923, at the time of the exchange of populations, both the Greek and Turkish governments agreed to consider them Greeks and transferred them to Greece. This was surely prudent; in the Middle East, it is much easier to change one's language than one's religion, and the Karamanlıs in Greece, however much discrimination they may have encountered, probably fused more easily with the Greeks than they would have done with the Turks.

Pending studies on the attitudes taken toward various questions by the Greek deputies who sat in successive Ottoman parliaments, and of content analyses of Greek publications in different parts of the empire, it is difficult to make definitive statements about the political views of Ottoman Greeks, but one point may be made. Not all Greeks, whether in the empire or even in the kingdom, thought in terms of unification. Partly because of growing tensions with the Bulgarians and other Slavs, and partly because of the favorable position of Greeks in the empire, some Greeks aimed for a state that would guarantee the rights of all the ethnicities in the empire. The Society of Constantinople propagated such views: "During the first years of its operations, the organization made considerable headway in the middle-class community of Constantinopolitan Greeks, but there is little evidence of its impact on the lower middle class, the working class, and the population of the countryside." Ultimately, it foundered on the intransigence of the Young Turks' nationalism and on the increasing tensions brought about by successive wars between Greece and Turkey.[60]

The Greek community in the Ottoman Empire was shattered by the disastrous war of 1918–1922. However, the survivors—more fortunate than some other peoples—found a new home in the Kingdom of Greece. Their contribution to its development falls outside the scope of this book.[61]

Notes

1. Abraham Galanté, *Turcs et Juifs* (Istanbul: Haim, Rozio, 1932), pp. 94–101.

2. See Mark Epstein, "The Leadership of the Ottoman Jews," in Benjamin Braude and Bernard Lewis, *Christians and Jews in the Ottoman Empire*, (New York: Holmes and Meier Publishers, 1982), vol. 1, pp. 101–15, and Joseph R. Hacker, "Ottoman Policy Towards the Jews," in ibid., vol. 1, pp. 117–26.

3. A. Üner Turgay, "Trade and Merchants in Nineteenth-century Trabzon," in Braude and Lewis, op. cit., p. 288. On the wheat trade, see Lütfi Gücer, "Istanbul iaşesi . . ." *Istanbul Üniversitesi Iktisat Fakültesi Mecmuasi* (Istanbul University, Journal of the Faculty of Economics), vol. 2 (1949–50): 397–411, translated in Charles Issawi, *The Economic History of Turkey* (Chicago: University of Chicago Press, 1980), pp. 26–31; see also John H. Lampe and Marvin R. Jackson, *Balkan Economic History, 1550–1950* (Bloomington: Indiana University Press, 1982), p. 83.

4. C. M. Woodhouse, *Modern Greece, A Short History* (London: Faber and Faber, 1986), p. 126.

5. Nicolas Svoronos, *Histoire de la Grèce Moderne* (Paris: Presses Universitaires de France, 1980), p. 24.

6. L. S. Stavrianos, *The Balkans Since 1453* (New York: Holt, Rinehart, and Winston, 1958), pp. 198–213. As early as the fifteenth century, the Greeks "seem to have been the most closely involved with the foreigner"; they controlled the guilds concerned with navigation and shipbuilding: they supplied both translators to the merchants and dragomans to the foreign embassies; and they were prominent in the wheat and coin trade. See Robert Mantran, "Foreign Merchants and Minorities in Istanbul During the Sixteenth and Seventeenth Centuries," in Braude and Lewis, op. cit., vol. 1, pp. 130–33.

7. Stavrianos, op. cit., p. 107; Bernard Lewis, *The Emergence of Modern Turkey* (London: Oxford University Press, 1961), pp. 85–86.

8. Stavrianos, op. cit., pp. 98, 109–12, 146–53.

9. Richard Clogg, "The Greek Millet in the Ottoman Empire," in Braude and Lewis, op. cit., vol. 1, p. 188.

10. See Svoronos, op. cit., pp. 39, 59, 72; and Issawi, op. cit., p. 18.

11. For Iran see Charles Issawi, *The Economic History of Iran* (Chicago: University of Chicago Press, 1971), pp. 57–62 and sources cited therein.

12. The following paragraphs draw heavily on Charles Issawi, "The Transformation of the Economic Position of the *Millets*," in Braude and Lewis, op. cit., vol. 1, pp. 261–85 and idem, *Economic History of Turkey*, p. 57.

13. See dispatches from the Austrian Internuncio in Constantinople of 11 and 25 January 1802, translated in Issawi, *Economic History of Turkey*, p. 57. In the eighteenth century, Greeks from Chios (including the Ralli

family) and elsewhere had a far-flung trade, with branches ranging from Amsterdam to Vienna, Odessa, and Moscow, and in various European and Ottoman Mediterranean ports.

14. A. Gündüz Okçün, *Yillari Osmanli Sanayii, 1913–1915* [Ottoman Industry, The Years 1913–1915] (Ankara: Ankara Universitesi Siyasal Bilgiler Facultesi, 1970), passim.

15. Cited by O. G. Indzhikyan, *Burzhuaziya Osmanskoi Imperii* (Erevan: Izd-vo Arm.SSR, 1977), p. 166.

16. Issawi, "Transformation," p. 263, which gives the breakdown by branches.

17. Great Britain, *Accounts and Papers*, 1873, vol. 68, "Turkey" and Bursa, "Trade Report, 1858," Foreign Office Archives, FO 195/64.

18. See Issawi, *Economic History of Turkey*, pp. 50–52.

19. S. D. Chapman, "The International Houses," *Journal of European Economic History*, vol. 6, no. 1 (Spring, 1977).

20. Indzhikyan, op. cit., pp. 212.

21. Ibid., p. 211, which gives the breakdown by branches.

22. Donald Quataert, "Ottoman Reform and Agriculture in Anatolia, 1876–1908," Ph.D. dissertation, UCLA, 1973, p. 68.

23. A. A. Bryer, cited in R. Clogg, "The Greek *Millet*," in Braude and Lewis, op. cit., vol. 1, p. 206.

24. Turgay, in Braude and Lewis, *Christians and Jews*, pp. 308–10.

25. Dispatch of 16 April 1850, FO 78/833, reproduced in Issawi, *Economic History of Turkey*, pp. 155–56.

26. Stavrianos, op. cit., p. 480.

27. Despatch of 31 December 1842, FO 78/533, reproduced in Issawi, *Economic History of Turkey*, op. cit., p. 166; Turgay, op. cit., p. 292.

28. See table in Issawi, op. cit., p. 176.

29. For examples see Turgay, op. cit., and Indzhikyan, op. cit., p. 212.

30. See table in Indzhikyan, op. cit., p. 214. I suspect that the relatively better showing of Armenians in the legal field may have been due to their greater mastery of Turkish.

31. There is no reference to personnel in Donald Blaisdell, *European Financial Control in the Ottoman Empire* (New York: Columbia University Press, 1929).

32. See table in Carter V. Findley, *Ottoman Civil Officialdom* (Princeton: Princeton University Press, 1989), p. 103; see also idem, *Bureaucratic Reform in the Ottoman Empire* (Princeton: Princeton University Press, 1980), pp. 205–12.

33. See table in idem, *Ottoman Civil*, p. 168.

34. Ibid., pp. 264–65.

35. Alexis Alexandris, *The Greek Minority of Istanbul* (Athens: Center for Asia Minor Studies, 1983), pp. 28–30, 43; Comnenos served as ambassador in St. Petersburg. See R. Davison, "The *Millets* as Agents of Change," in Braude and Lewis, op. cit., vol. 1, p. 326.

36. Quataert, op. cit., table on p. 85 and pp. 68–110.

37. For a breakdown see A. Synvet, *Les Grecs de l'Empire Ottoman: Etude Statistique et Ethnographique* (Constantinople: Imprimerie de "l'Orient illustré," 1878), pp. 32–33, 80–83, translated in Issawi, *Economic History of Turkey*, pp. 60–61.

38. See Alexandris, op. cit., pp. 326–31.

39. Of the estimated 2.1 million Greeks in the empire in 1897, some 300,000 lived in Constantinople and 100,000 in Smyrna; another 100,000 to 200,000 probably lived in the smaller towns.

40. For examples, see Indzhikyan, op. cit., pp. 60–63.

41. A. J. Sussnitzki, "Zum Gliederung wirtschaftslicher Arbeit," translated in Charles Issawi, *The Economic History of the Middle East* (Chicago: University of Chicago Press, 1966), pp. 114–25.

42. W. F. Brück, "Türkische Baumwollwirtschaft," *Probleme der Weltwirtschaft*, no. 29 (Jena, 1919).

43. Report on Trade, FO 78/796; Reply to Questionnaire FO 78/1525; ibid., FO 78/1533; see also R. Davison, "The *Millets* as Agents of Change," op. cit., pp. 324–25.

44. Sir Charles Eliot, *Turkey in Europe* (reprint, New York: Barnes and Noble, 1965), p. 153.

45. W. M. Ramsay, *Impressions of Turkey* (London: Hodder and Stoughton, 1897) pp. 130–31. The same connection with railways was noted 20 years later by Karl Dietrich, *Hellenism in Asia Minor* (New York: Oxford University Press, 1918), pp. 46–49.

46. For a bitter Turkish account of conditions in the Smyrna market, see Halit Ziya Uşakligil, *Kırk Yıl* [40 years] (5 vols., Istanbul, 1936), vol. 2, pp. 14–16; translated in Issawi, *The Economic History of Turkey*, pp. 72–73.

47. For details, see Athanase Politis, *L'Hellénisme et l'Egypte Moderne*, 2 vols. (Paris: F. Alcan, 1929–1930), vol. 2, pp. 401–90.

48. Lord Cromer, *Modern Egypt*, 2 vols. (New York: Macmillan, 1908), vol. 2, p. 250.

49. See Charles Issawi, "The Tabriz-Trabzon Trade, 1830–1900," *International Journal of Middle Eastern Studies*, vol. 1, no. 1 (1970).

50. See various documents reproduced or translated in Issawi, *The Economic History of Iran*, pp. 97–109.

51. Ibid., pp. 231–32.

52. Idem, *The Fertile Crescent, 1800–1914* (New York: Oxford University Press, 1988), p. 25.

53. Ibid., pp. 279, 296–97.

54. Great Britain, *Accounts and Papers*, 1900, Report No. 2441, "Beirut."

55. For a list, see Alexandris, op. cit., pp. 324–25.

56. For an account, see Hrachya Adjarian, "Hayots dere Osmanian," *Bamber Erevani Hamalsarani* (Erevan, 1967), translated in Issawi, *The Economic History of Turkey*, pp. 62–65; R. Davison, op. cit., pp. 323–24.

57. See Metin And, *A History of Theater and Popular Entertainment in*

Turkey (Ankara: Forum Yayinlari, 1963–64), pp. 67–80. An interesting point may be mentioned: In 1913, the number of daily papers published in Constantinople in Greek was 6 and of periodicals, 12; the corresponding figures in Armenian were 6 and 17. In the provinces there were, however, 19 Greek papers (mainly in Smyrna) and 17 Armenian—see Ahmed Emin [Yalman], *The Development of Modern Turkey as Measured by its Press* (New York: Columbia University Press, 1914), pp. 117–18.

58. In the forthcoming volume edited by Dimitri Gondicas and Charles Issawi, *Ottoman Greeks in the Age of Nationalism* (Princeton: Darwin Press).

59. Ibid.

60. On this subject, see Alexandris, op. cit., pp. 36–44.

61. See D. Pentzopoulos, *The Balkan Exchange of Minorities and its Impact upon Greece* (The Hague: Mouton, 1962).

SEVEN

THE COSTS OF THE
FRENCH REVOLUTION

In 1989 the world celebrated, with much enthusiasm, the two hundredth anniversary of the French Revolution. In this it continued a tradition that was begun by the finest poets of their age—Blake, Wordsworth, Coleridge, Southey, Byron, Shelley, Schiller, and, in his cooler and more detached way, Goethe, as witnessed by his remarks at the battle of Valmy on the dawn of a new era and in some conversations with Eckermann. Wordsworth's

> Bliss was it in that dawn to be alive
> But to be young was very Heaven

is very well known; Byron's

> . . . Revolution
> Alone can save the earth from hell's pollution

is equally characteristic of the period, and Shelley is full of quotable lines.

Not only poets were thus affected; Charles James Fox exclaimed: "How much the greatest event it is that ever happened in the world! And how much the best." Several other statesmen such as Sheridan were also favorably inclined; even Pitt was, for a couple of years, somewhat charitable.

The achievements of the Revolution were great and have received their due. But like all human events, it had its costs, which have attracted far less attention. It seems worthwhile to point out and assess these costs. To what extent they offset the positive aspects must be left to the reader to judge.

The first and most obvious was the loss of life through Revolutionary violence. First there was the terror of 1793–1794. An eminent French historian, Pierre Goubert, sums it up as follows: "Paris, where over 2,000 persons were guillotined in 16 months. Of the 14,000 victims who have been fully identified, less than 15 percent were nobles and clergymen and nearly 60 percent workers and peasants. Adding the killings in Vendée, the number of victims was well over a hundred thousand, perhaps close to twice that figure. Passion, hatred and folly contributed as much as national necessity, which cannot be ignored." And, of course, there were many executions, and many more deportations, after the fall of Robespierre.

These figures are appalling, but to keep them in perspective they should be compared to France's total population of about 27 million. And it is worth recalling Shelley's admonition, in the preface to *The Revolt of Islam,* not to condemn the Revolution just "because a nation of men who had been dupes and slaves for centuries were incapable of conducting themselves with the wisdom and tranquillity of freemen as soon as some of their fetters were partially loosened." Moreover, a certain logic of all revolutions should be noted. Once they have begun—usually in violence—they evoke counterrevolutionary violence, which makes further violence unavoidable if the revolutionary momentum is to be maintained.

To this should be added the casualties of the Revolutionary and Napoleonic wars, probably over 1 million Frenchmen—a figure calculated by a count of casualties in Napoléon's wars and checked by the deficiency of 1 million men compared to women in the age-group of 20–59 years in a reconstituted population pyramid of France for 1815. The combined casualties of France's enemies were probably of a similar order of magnitude, and losses among civilians on both sides must have also been very high. War was not a novelty in France, and the losses involved in the wars of Louis XIV, although distinctly smaller, were not of a different order of magnitude. But, unlike the Bourbon wars, the Revolutionary and Napoleonic wars did not result in any permanent extension of France's frontiers. In fact, she lost her remaining colonies, which had been an important source of income (discussed later in this chapter), and her fleet was wiped out. Again to quote Goubert: "After Aboukir, mourning for Trafalgar would be observed by our sailors for over a century."

In addition to the quantitative, there were qualitative losses. The terror was responsible for the deaths of Lavoisier, Europe's greatest scientist; André Chénier, France's leading poet; Vicq d'Azyr, her leading physician; Condorcet, her leading philosopher; and Olympe de Gouges, her most prominent feminist. Other notable writers—among them Chateaubriand, Mme de Staël, Rivarol, and, eventually, Benjamin Constant—went into exile. Moreover, the rigors of the Revolution and Napoléon's censorship had a chilling effect on literature, and no noteworthy poetry or prose—except for Napoléon's own despatches—was written. On the other hand, the gorgeous flowering of French literature in the 1820s certainly owes something to the Revolutionary glow as well as to English Romanticism, which in turn had felt the same impulse.

Another loss, minor and unnoticed, may be mentioned: under the Directory a very large number of castles and churches, including some fine monuments, were demolished and their remains carted away. However, considering the prodigious architectural wealth of France, one need not attach too much importance to this particular loss.

An authoritative, and sympathetic, historian, Charles Gillispie, states: "Indeed in what is now called high culture [philosophy, literature, fine arts, music] the quarter century between 1789 and 1815 is to be graphed as the bottom of a trough between the elevated plateaus of the Enlightenment and the 19th century." But there was an important exception. As Gillispie immediately adds: "Only in one domain were French names at the forefront in the world at large, and that domain was science," more particularly in physics and biology, but also in chemistry and other sciences. Beginning around the middle of the eighteenth century, the Royal Academy of Science had done superb work in both encouraging individual scientists and organizing scientific work. Several specialized "grandes écoles" were founded, such as Mines, Génie, and Ponts et Chaussées. The Jacobins were hostile to the mathematical, mechanical sciences and in 1793 suppressed the Academy and, as noted, executed many of its leading members. But, under the Directory, the Academy was reconstituted under the name of Institut de France, and in addition Polytechnique and other Grandes Écoles were founded. Napoléon—the only head of government before the twentieth century who had received a technical education—also greatly encouraged science. The brilliant younger scientists (Ampère, Fresnel, Fourier, Poisson, Cuvier, Sadi Carnot, and others), as well as survivors of the Royal Academy (Laplace, Monge, and Berthollet), rendered great services to the French state, ranging from the production of gunpowder to the survey of Egypt.

The Convention and Directory also had far-reaching plans—many taken over from the reformers of the Ancien Régime—for universal primary and secondary education, and in 1795 an early version of the École Normale was established for teacher training. But Napoléon was far from enthusiastic, and implementation of these schemes had to wait for several decades. The initial influence of the Revolution on education was surely disruptive, but this was soon rectified, and the tendencies prevailing under the old régime—notably nationalization and modernization of education—were soon resumed. In R. R. Palmer's words: "For the mass of the population, at the level of elementary schooling, very little had changed; the rate of basic literacy in 1820, as already noted, stood about where it might have been expected without the Revolution, on a curve that had been rising since the time of Louis XIV, and probably before." But more was done for secondary education.

The major political costs of the Revolution were overcentralization and the splitting of the country into Red and Black. As Tocqueville pointed out, centralization had begun long before and had been vigorously pursued by Richelieu and his successors. As Tocqueville also saw, the Jacobins and Napoléon carried the process much further, partly no doubt because of the wars. It is generally agreed that France became overcentralized and was deprived of the invigorating presence of strong provincial governments, as in the United States, Germany, and, later, Britain. Only in the last few decades has a serious attempt been made to decentralize France's government, its educational system, and other aspects of economic and social activity.

Some of the initial measures taken by the Revolution—particularly the persecution of the priests—and the civil war of 1793 split France into two irreconcilable camps: the secular Left, consisting mainly of bourgeois and urban workers, with its center in Paris, and the religious Right, consisting of aristocrats, bourgeois, and peasants and drawing its support from the provinces. The resulting clashes punctuate the history of the nineteenth century: the Three Glorious Days of July 1830, the February Revolution of 1848, the June Revolution of 1848 followed by the coup d'état of Napoléon III in 1851, and the Commune uprising of 1871. As Flaubert pointed out in *L'éducation sentimentale*, in 1848 everyone followed the tricolor, but each party was committed to only one of its constituent colors. Again and again the revolutionary groups in Paris tried to impose their will on the country, as they had done in 1793, but as the century wore on, the weight of the provinces bore them down. The last such conflict was in 1968 and was far more peaceful than its predecessors. Since then the two sides have come together to an unprecedented degree, and it does not seem unwarranted to say that by now the wounds have healed. But for nearly 200 years, they caused much pain to the body politic.

Of course there were some very important political gains, many of which are widely known and which will consequently just be mentioned here. First and foremost, there was national unity: one law covered the whole of France, instead of a multitude of provincial regulations; feudal dues were abolished; taxes became uniform; and all internal barriers, including tolls, were removed. The Code Napoléon—work on which had started well before the Consulate—became a model for mankind, and so did the excellent metric system. Justice became more humane. Protestants and Jews were granted political equality with Catholics. Administration was streamlined—and became at once less expensive and more effective. Above all, the principle of constitutional limitations on executive power was accepted and, although at first almost wholly ignored in practice, eventually established itself in French political life. More immediately, social mobility greatly increased and careers became more open to talents.

Even these splendid achievements had their darker side. The grip of the state on the individual was tightened to a degree never achieved by the absolute monarchs. In particular, universal conscription—another French innovation that was widely adopted abroad—constituted a heavy burden. But, on balance, the vast majority of present-day observers would surely agree that, in the political field, the gains of the Revolution outweighed its costs.

In the economic field, however, the picture is very different. In the first place, the Revolutionary disruption and the almost uninterrupted wars represented a huge cost, both in the form of direct expenditures and in the opportunity costs of the hundreds of thousands of men mobilized and resources allocated to war purposes. According to Peter Mathias and Patrick O'Brien, between 1785 and 1807–1808 the share of France's commodity output that was appropriated as taxes went up by 30 percent—the corresponding figure for Britain being over 50 percent. However, because of mass mobilization, the opportunity cost in France must have risen much more sharply than in Britain. Far more important, these events led to the retardation of economic growth and a sharp deterioration in the position of France relative to that of Britain, its only rival for hegemony.

Considerable quantitative work has been done in the last 40 years on the evolution of the French economy, which may be summarized as follows. In the "long seventeenth century" France suffered greatly from the civil wars, Louis XIV's wars, and the emigration of Protestants following the Revocation of the Edict of Nantes. As a result, its economy underwent considerable retardation compared to that of its main rivals, first the Netherlands and then Britain. From 1715 to 1789, however, France progressed at least as fast as Britain, no doubt partly because of its recovery from a lower level. Its foreign trade grew distinctly more rapidly than that of Britain. So did its agriculture—according to some estimates by 50 percent more, though this figure should not be pressed too hard, because of the shakiness of the statistics on which it is based. Yet there was more agricultural innovation in Britain than in France. Even in industry, the overall French rate of growth was higher, thanks mainly to the excellent performance of the woolen, linen, silk, and iron industries, while Britain did better in coal, shipbuilding, and, above all, cotton, where the new inventions were centered. By and large, it is agreed that the volume of physical production grew more rapidly in France, but this was at least partly offset by the far better performance of the financial and services sector in Britain. There also seems little doubt that whereas, in 1789, taken as a whole, the economy of France was much larger than that of Britain, per capita income in the latter was higher. It should be added that in both countries population rose at what were then high rates, with that of England and Wales being slightly above that of France.

The French Revolution, then, had a sharply adverse effect on the economy. The political upheavals, civil wars, confiscations, and currency depreciation disrupted business. Interest rates rose sharply, and investment probably declined. But these factors pale into insignificance compared to the effects of the foreign wars. The most immediate and harmful effect was on foreign trade. Within a very few years the Royal Navy had swept French ships and trade off the seas, and the British had taken France's colonies; simultaneously Haiti, "The Pearl of the Antilles," revolted and became independent. Subsequently blockades and counterblockades, Napoléon's Continental System, and the British Orders in Council practically eliminated

France's overseas trade. The economic loss was most severe in trade with the Americas, which had been France's main overseas market, but it was equally dramatic in the Near East, also an important client. Before the Revolution, France accounted for more than half of the Ottoman Empire's trade with Europe; by 1815 France's share was negligible, and it was not until the 1840s that it again rose to a significant proportion.

The shrinkage in trade had cut deeply into industry. Many of France's leading manufacturing centers, such as Bordeaux, Nantes, Rouen, and Marseilles, were port cities that catered mainly to foreign markets and drew their raw materials (sugar, tobacco, cotton, etc.) from abroad. The resulting collapse was so great that Crouzet, followed by Wallerstein, uses the terms "definitive deindustrialization or pastoralization of vast regions—with, in many parts of France and the Low Countries, an appreciable transfer of capital from commerce and industry to agriculture." This was partly offset by the growth of the cotton spinning and weaving industries— which had begun to import machines from England as early as 1770—and of the metal-using and chemical industries. All these branches benefited greatly from the Continental Blockade, often at the expense of other European producers. The woolen industry, which had suffered greatly under the Revolution, also revived under Napoléon. For total industrial production, Crouzet suggests a decline from 100 in the 1780s to 60 in 1800 and a recovery to at most 90 by 1810. In the meantime Britain was furiously industrializing and supplying overseas markets and, by 1815, had acquired a commanding lead that would not be overcome until the last few years, even though French industrial productivity advanced almost as fast as British. Already in 1801 Pitt, in a speech of November 3, had seen the situation very clearly: what France had gained in territory it had lost "in population, in commerce, in capital and in habits of industry."

It may be argued that British technological superiority would have ensured a similar outcome regardless of political and military developments, but this does not seem to be the opinion of most economic historians—among other reasons because the French were introducing many British machines and making others of their own. Well over a hundred years ago, Thiers stated: "We did not win the battle of Trafalgar. We did not remain masters of the seas and do not have 200 million consumers like England. Here is all the secret of our inferiority." But he should have gone back beyond Trafalgar, to the early 1790s.

As for agriculture, the main result of the Revolution and the subsequent wars was that of mass conscription and the acquisition of much land by the peasants. The loss of manpower must have adversely affected agricultural production and was not compensated by mechanization. The effects of redistribution of land were complex. Well before other European countries, France became a land of small peasant proprietors. This probably made its farming less responsive to agricultural improvement, such as was carried out by British landlords and Prussian junkers. Grain yields per acre on comparable land were distinctly lower in France than in England; moreover, for most cereals, yields per acre seem to have declined. Against that, however, must be set the social benefits of diffused and much less unequal landownership—a fact to which, perhaps more than any other, France owed its social stability throughout its successive nineteenth-century revolutions.

Peasant ownership is also generally believed to have been a major factor in sharply reducing the birth rate in France, the first such instance in the modern era. At the same time, the wars were not only killing off many potential husbands and fathers but probably leading to the postponement of many marriages, with a consequent decline in fertility. This resulted in a marked slowdown in population growth. From 1781 to 1789 France had nearly three times as many inhabitants as Britain (26.5 million against 9.4 million) but from 1815 to 1824 just over twice as many (30.5 million against 13.9 million), and by the end of the century, the two countries were dead even. This naturally meant that France's *overall* rate of growth was slowed down compared to that of its neighbors—Britain, Germany, and Italy—and that its total economic and military power was correspondingly reduced, a fact of which Frenchmen became painfully aware. But it does not follow that the French per capita rate of growth was reduced. The following table suggests that, after a sharp drop during the Revolutionary and Napoleonic period, the French rate of growth was as rapid as the British. One caveat is necessary: table 7.1 shows total *commodity* output, not gross national product—that is, it excludes the service sector. This was far larger in Britain than in France, and it meant that per capita incomes were also distinctly higher. Thanks partly to imports financed by such international services as banking, shipping, and insurance, the British had more goods at their disposal than the French and enjoyed a higher level of living.

TABLE 7.1. Per Capita Commodity Output in Pounds Sterling

Years	Great Britain	France
1781–1789	6.9	7.94–9.53
1815–1824	12.27	9.22–11.31
1865–1874	17.64	17.92–19.33
1905–1913	21.53	21.89–22.43

The two figures for France show the results of converting at prices based on British output and on French output, respectively. (P. O'Brien and C. Keyder, *Economic Growth in Britain and France, 1780–1914* {London, 1978}, p.61.)

Slower population growth also had the effect of sharply reducing rural migration to the cities, so that France remained much less urbanized than Britain, Belgium, or Germany. This retarded industrialization by reducing both the available supply of workers (and therefore presumably preventing wages from falling) and the number of urban consumers. But here, too, the social effects were beneficial, for France was spared some of the horrors of early industrialization. The urban slums of Paris, Lille, and Lyons may have been as bad as those of Britain, but they were far more restricted. Most nineteenth-century French observers of England, including such admirers as Tocqueville and Taine, were horrified by the condition of the urban working class and the much greater inequality prevailing, and against the many debit entries attributable to the French Revolution must be set this large credit item.

Let us now consider, very briefly, the external effects of the Revolution. In his *Civilization and Ethics*, Albert Schweitzer provides an arresting image:

The French Revolution is a snowstorm falling upon trees in blossom. A transformation which promises great things is in progress, but everywhere softly and slowly. Extraordinarily valuable results are being prepared in the thoughts of men. Provided that circumstances remain even tolerably near the normal, there stands before humanity in Europe an extraordinarily desirable development. But in place of that there sets in a chaotic period of history in which the will-to-progress has to cease more or less completely from its work, and becomes a bewildered spectator.

The eighteenth century had been the age of enlightened despotism or, in Lord Acton's phrase, "the era of repentant monarchy."

Almost everywhere the monarchs and their ministers—Frederick the Great in Prussia, Maria Theresa and Joseph II in Austria, Charles III and Florida Blanca in Spain, Joseph I and Pombal in Portugal, as well as the rulers of Tuscany and some other small states in Italy—had achieved much progress. Even in Russia, Catherine the Great had introduced some reforms. In the maritime countries—Britain, the Netherlands, and the United States—much more had been achieved. The nobility and the clergy had been deprived of some of their privileges, though only to a minor extent. Administration had become more humane, and in many places torture was abolished—or at least discredited. Toleration increased greatly, and the status of minorities—Protestants, Catholics, Jews—was significantly improved; paradoxically, the Jesuits were expelled from many countries, because of their intolerance. Steps were taken to extend education. Taxation became less arbitrary and attempts were made to develop the economy.

By contrast, the six or seven decades following the Revolution present a bleak picture. The rulers of Europe had been thoroughly shaken, and reaction replaced reform. Even in Britain, the movement to reform Parliament and other institutions was set back for four decades.

It could be countered that the Revolution may well have scared the ruling classes, but it surely radicalized the masses and increased their ardor. This is shown by the numerous revolts and revolutions that broke out in many parts of Europe after the Restoration. However, almost all of these revolutions, including those of 1848, were miserable failures. Under Metternich and his allies, reaction had the upper hand and it was only in the second half of the nineteenth century that constitutional reforms were slowly carried out and liberalism began to flourish on the Continent.

One other important external effect of the Revolution should be noted: nationalism. The Revolution, the allied invasion, and the subsequent conquests greatly stimulated French nationalism. The same effect was soon felt in neighboring countries, especially Germany where, beginning with Fichte, nationalism arose in reaction to French domination. To pass a summary judgment on such a profound and complex phenomenon would be absurd, but one cannot help feeling that its effects were predominately malign.

This leads to a final question, which will make any respectable historian shudder: was the French Revolution necessary? Would not its main achievements have come about anyway, in the course of a slow evolution: centralization, constitutional limitations on the monarchy, the acquisition of a greater share of power by the bourgeoisie, and a slowly widening suffrage, religious toleration, judicial and administrative reform, and the establishment of a legal system more favorable to capitalist expansion? The example of France's neighbors, Britain, the Netherlands, Switzerland, and eventually Scandinavia—not to mention the United States, which was in an altogether different category—suggests that such an evolution was by no means impossible. So does Tocqueville, who wrote: "Si elle [the Revolution] n'eût pas eu lieu, le vieil édifice social n'en serait pas moins tombé partout, ici plus tôt, là plus tard; seulement il aurait continué à tomber pièce à pièce, au lieu de s'effondrer tout à coup. La Révolution à achevé soudainement, par un effort convulsif et douloureux, sans transition, sans précaution, sans égards, ce qui se serait achevé peu à peu de soi-même à la longue." The combined effects of the development of industry, commerce, and finance and of the ideas of the Enlightenment might well, by themselves, have abolished feudalism and created a political and social environment more favorable to capitalism. Even the transfer of the land, one of the Revolution's most spectacular achievements, had begun much earlier; as George Lefebvre points out, in 1789 the bourgeois probably owned as much land as the nobility.

However, some important differences between France and its neighbors should be noted. First, commerce, industry, and finance played a distinctly smaller role in its economy than in those of the other countries, and the agrarian aristocracy was correspondingly stronger. The French aristocracy was much more reluctant to replenish its ranks from commerce and finance than was, say, the British—though it did recruit many members of the legal profession. France's Catholic church was far more powerful than the Protestant churches of other countries—though it should be noted that, in 1789, a substantial majority of the clergy (the lower ranks) voted to join the Third Estate, thus making possible the formation of the General Assembly, consisting of the three orders, and that many of the Cahiers presented by the clergy were radical in tone.

The fiscal difficulties of France were also far more serious than those of its neighbors. Attempts to regain solvency by increasing taxation and reducing expenditure had been repeatedly frustrated in the face of the extravagance of the Court and the refusal of the privileged classes to bear their share. The efforts of a distinguished group of reformers, including Turgot and Necker, had failed. In 1769,

Burke—later the most implacable critic of the French Revolution—had stated in his *Observations on a Late Publication intituled "The Present State of the Nation"*:

> Under such extreme straightness and distraction labours the whole body of their finances, so far does their charge outrun their supply in every particular, that no man, I believe, who has considered their affairs with any degree of attention or information but must hourly look for some extraordinary convulsion in that whole system: the effect of which on France, and even on all Europe, it is difficult to conjecture.

And that was before the American War had greatly increased France's debt and fiscal burden.

Lastly, and most germanely, the Netherlands and England had had their revolutions—the first in the form of the revolt against Spain and the second in 1641 and 1688. Perhaps a revolution was a precondition for the emergence of a bourgeois, constitutional regime. Perhaps only a revolution could have shattered the old structures and produced a bourgeois society—though it should be immediately added that many influential contemporary historians emphatically deny that this was the result of the Revolution.

After two hundred years, the Revolution has worked itself out. The reforms and transformations it set out to achieve, and the ideas it sought to propagate, have long been accepted. For many decades now the Left has looked to other sources of inspiration. Similarly, the costs of the Revolution have been fully absorbed. The breach between the Red and the Black has been filled up, and France is no more divided today than is any other Western democracy. There has been some decentralization. The economic retardation caused by the Revolution has been fully made up, and France now stands at least level with Britain and very close to Germany. The 1789 Revolution was one of the greatest events in history, and, like other great events, it had its cost. Some of these were surely avoidable but others may well not have been. Whether they were excessive must be judged by each individual observer, using his own particular scales, which are likely to give different readings on different days.[1]

Note

1. After this chapter had appeared in its original form, my attention was drawn, by Professor Albert O. Hirschman, to René Sédillot's *Le Coût de la Révolution française* (Paris, 1987), which covers, in greater detail, several of

the topics dealt with there. Although this book is based on different sources and often gives different figures (for instance, the human losses are put at about 2,000,000), by a strange quirk of fate not only are the conclusions in broad agreement but the titles are identical. On the whole, however, it is more negative. This coincidence is perhaps less surprising in view of the fact that Sédillot is described on the blurb as "économiste de formation, historien de vocation," a label that fits exactly me. All I can do is repeat the line in Ionesco's *La cantatrice chauve*: "Comme c'est curieux, comme c'est bizarre et quelle coincidence."

EIGHT

THE STRUGGLE FOR
LINGUISTIC HEGEMONY,
1780–1980

In its issue of January 26, 1980, the *Economist* carried the following comment: "After a long struggle, the French seem to have abandoned their efforts to stem the rising tide of the English language. . . . The government has quietly endorsed a plan which calls for an end to the competition with English. . . . His [Jacques Rigaud's] report, approved by senior cabinet ministers last month, recognized that, compared with English, French has come to look old-fashioned."

If this account is correct—and I am inclined to doubt it, having sat through many long sessions at the United Nations in which the French delegates criticized at length the inadequacy of the French translations of documents and the insufficient use of French at the UN—it marks the end of a long rivalry, at first latent and then overt and conscious, between the English and French languages for world supremacy. For more than 200 years English has been gaining ground in business and science, but only since the First World War has it taken its place alongside French as the language of diplomacy and international culture. Other languages have achieved temporary preeminence in certain fields. Italian was for several centuries the lingua franca of the Mediterranean; the Treaty of Kuchuk Kainarji, concluded by the Russians and Ottomans in 1774, was in Italian, and in certain parts of the Levant Italian was replaced by French only in the nineteenth century, during which German became the language of scholarship. But so far none has been able to challenge French or English as an international language.

A convenient point at which to start the study of this competition is Antoine de Rivarol's prizewinning essay, *Discours sur l'universalité de la langue française*, a subject set by the Academy of Berlin in 1783. The time and place are symbolic. Berlin was the capital of Frederick the Great, an ardent admirer of French culture, who wrote French verse, is reported to have said that Shakespeare was for "Redskins," and did not have much more use for German literature. Rivarol's was by no means the first essay of its kind—one can refer to Henri Estienne's *De la précellence du langage français*, written in the sixteenth century, Jean Le Laboureur's *Avantages de la langue française sur la langue latine* (1667), and other works—but it is the most complete and convincing.

In his attempt to explain how French became the leading language of Europe, Rivarol passes in review its potential rivals and shows their shortcomings. Some of these relate to sonority: German and English are too guttural, Spanish too bombastic, Italian too soft. Others relate to vocabulary: thus, German is too far removed from Latin to be acceptable to the rest of Europe. Still others relate to syntax—English syntax is odd and obscure—or to the spirit of the language. But the main reasons for the preponderance of French have been geographic, historical, political, social, and economic. German and Italian were handicapped by the disunity of their countries, and in addition Italy suffered from devastating invasions and the diversion of trade routes in the sixteenth century. The language of Spain, along with other aspects of its society, went into decline at the end of that century. The florescence of Italian literature was too early; it came before Europe was ready for it. That of England was too tardy: "From Chaucer until Shakespeare and Milton nothing transpires in this famous island, and its literature is not worth a glance." Shakespeare and Milton were not appreciated in their own country for nearly two centuries [*sic*], and by the time England began to shine in letters (Pope, Addison, Dryden) and in thought (Locke, Newton) it was too late: France had taken an unchallengeable lead.

For the French language had been favored by a wide variety of powerful factors—by its euphony and clarity (*"what is not clear is not French;* what is not clear is still English, Italian, Greek or Latin") and by its early unity, derived from the triumph of the Picard dialect which made it such an excellent instrument of prose ("and it is prose that gives a language domination"). French also benefited from its slow evolution over a thousand years. Already by the thirteenth and fourteenth centuries the language had reached a high level of perfection and, after the aberrant exuberance of Ronsard and other sixteenth-century poets, attained its final form under Malherbe. By then France had achieved primacy in a number of fields: military, political, and economic. (Indeed Rivarol could have emphasized much more strongly than he did that seventeenth-century France was a giant among nations. It was situated at the heart of Western Europe, between all the countries that counted: Spain, Italy, Britain, the Netherlands, and Germany. Its population of 20 million compared with about 15 million for Germany, 13 million for Italy, 10 million for Spain and Portugal, and 9 million for the British Isles. Its manufacturing and agricultural outputs were easily the largest in Europe and so was its trade. From the defeat of the Spaniards at Rocroi in 1643 until Blenheim in 1704, French armies were unbeaten. And French political power was commensurate with its economic and military strength.) Louis XIV made Paris the center of Europe and his court was illuminated by a matchless galaxy: Corneille, Racine, Molière, La Fontaine, Descartes, Pascal, and others. "Enfin l'Europe, lasse d'admirer et d'envier, voulut imiter: c'était un nouvel hommage"; and French customs and culture spread across the continent. The task was rendered easier by the French character—gay, gracious, pleasant, and polite, in contrast to the dry, taciturn, impatient English: "One can no more succeed in boring a Frenchman than in diverting an Englishman."

In the eighteenth century, although France suffered political misfortunes, its literature was enriched by Voltaire, Rousseau, and the Encyclopedists, and its attractiveness thereby further enhanced. Rivarol's essay concludes on a very hopeful note: "We still live on their glory, and we shall maintain it." Meanwhile "England, which witnessed our successes, does not share them. Her last war against us leaves her under the double eclipse of her literature and preponderance, and that war gave Europe a great spectacle: in it, we have seen a free people led by England to slavery and brought back to liberty by a young monarch. The history of America can henceforth be reduced to three periods: strangled by Spain, oppressed by England, and saved by France."

Rivarol's general picture is not overdrawn. Imitation Versailles had grown up in Schoenbrunn, Potsdam, and elsewhere; French was spoken by the upper classes in Poland and Russia, and French literature set the tone for the whole of Europe. One example, from just beyond the threshold of Europe, is suggestive. In 1809 the British ambassador in Constantinople apologized to George Canning for having drawn a treaty with Turkey in French. But, he explained, "Even if the negotiations had been carried on at Constantinople I should have found no Dragoman employed by the Porte sufficiently master of the English language to render himself responsible for affixing the signature of the Turkish Plenipotentiary to an instrument of so much importance." It may be added that in the archives in Vienna the correspondence between the Austrian Foreign Office and the Austrian ambassador at Constantinople, for the years 1800–1860, is almost entirely in French.

Several forces, however, were altering the balance between French and English; five were already at work when Rivarol wrote his essay, and a sixth was to explode a few years later. First, there was the founding of the French empire in Africa, which in the eighteenth century consisted only of a few trading posts in Senegal but was eventually to produce several millions of francophones. Second, and far more powerful, was the French Revolution, followed by the Napolenoic conquests, which in many ways helped to spread the French language and culture. There was the large-scale emigration of noblemen and royalists, thousands of whom earned a living as teachers of French in various parts of Europe or America, while others—like Rivarol himself—wrote and published abroad in French, and still others put to use the military or civilian skills they had acquired at home. They were followed some 20 years later by demobilized officers and soldiers from Napoleon's armies, who offered their services in many parts of the world, including Turkey, Egypt, and places farther east. French armies marched all over Europe, and their presence must have had on many a youngster the intoxicating effect described by Heinrich Heine in *Das Buch Le Grand*. In the countries annexed by France, the inhabitants had more solid inducements to learn its language.

But perhaps the most powerful stimulus to the preeminence of French was that it became, and remained for more than a century, the language of revolution and the inspiration of national liberation—even where, as in Spain, Germany, and elsewhere, liberation was directed against French rule. In his *Thoughts on French Affairs*, Edmund Burke had this to say about the revolutionary newspapers: "There are thirty of them in Paris alone. The language diffuses them more widely than the English, though the English too are much read. . . . They are like a battery, in which the stroke of any one ball produces no great effect, but the amount of continual repetition is decisive. Let us only suffer any person to tell us his story, morning and evening, but for one twelve month, and he will become our master."

While France thus captured at one stroke the imagination and sympathy of the Left, the factors that had earlier ensured its primacy in the upper circles of society continued to operate: the political and economic strength of France; its dazzling literary, artistic, and, for a long time, scientific activity; and the unique attraction of Paris and its way of life. To this day French has held its place as the language of good food, good wine, and lovemaking. In the nineteenth century, French spread well beyond the confines of Europe, becoming the leading cultural language of Latin America and the Near and Middle East. One is accustomed to think of French as the language of the elite in the Balkans, Turkey, the Levant, Egypt, and Iran. But it comes as a surprise to learn that French was the predominant language in Iraq, which was so strongly under British commercial and political influence. The British consul in Baghdad stated in February 1905 that "in Baghdad almost every educated man can speak and understand French." A month later, however, he was to report that the head of the French-backed Jewish Schools (Alliance Israélite) wanted to introduce English at Baghdad and Basra. "They find it necessary for commercial purposes."

Commerce was indeed tipping the scales in favor of English, but it operated together with industry and empire. Rivarol had of course noticed England's commercial activity, "ramified in the four parts of the world"; he regarded it as a source of weakness, since Britain could be wounded in a thousand different ways, "and it is never wanting for causes of war." But during the Revolutionary and Napoleonic wars, British sea power destroyed French overseas trade and gave Britain a commanding lead which it was not to lose until the middle of the present century. In 1840, the United Kingdom accounted for about one third of world trade, compared to one tenth for France and one twelfth for the United States, and by 1870 its share had risen to 40 percent, slowly declining thereafter. This was partly due to British maritime supremacy; in 1850 Britain owned 52 percent of the world's merchant navy, and as late as 1910 the figure was still as high as 46 percent. English soon became the main language of maritime navigation and is now used almost exclusively in air traffic all over the world.

But Britain's trade owed even more to the Industrial Revolution, which it pioneered and carried to maturity. In 1840–1850 Britain produced a half, or more, of the world's output of machine-made cotton textiles, iron, and coal; owned well over a third of the world's railways and steam-powered machinery; and was by far the largest producer of engineering products and builder of railways. It was only natural, therefore, that the language of the "workshop of the world" should become that of technology. And since British science was ahead of that of any other country (except, for some decades, Germany, and later the United States), English also became the leading scientific language. In addition, English began to make small inroads into the stronghold of French: the domain of letters and polite society. One can contrast the exclusive use of French in the aristocratic circles of Saint Petersburg in *War and Peace* with the anglicisms that crop up in *Anna Karenina*; it is well known that Tolstoy was deeply influenced by Dickens, though he had his reservations regarding Shakespeare, Thackeray, and George Eliot. Still earlier, the English Romantics had made their mark on all European literatures, including French. For instance, it is interesting to contrast Rivarol's condescending remarks about Shakespeare with Hugo's unbounded admiration for him. Down to the present day, English literature, science, and arts have flourished with undiminished vitality, and one can surmise that its far larger vocabulary has also helped the English language to forge ahead of French.

The change had not passed unnoticed. In 1873 the distinguished Swiss scientist, Alphonse de Candolle, in his *Histoire des sciences et des savants depuis deux siècles*, indulged in some linguistic futurology and raised the question of which modern language would be scientifically "dominant in the Twentieth Century." His answer was clear. English had the right mixture of Germanic and Latin words and structures, would soon be spoken by a majority of the civilized world, and was "adapted to modern tendencies," more specifically technology, science, and business. By 1970, "the English language will have advanced from 77 to 860 millions. The German language will have advanced from 62 to 124 millions. The French language will have advanced from $40\frac{1}{2}$ to $89\frac{1}{2}$ millions. The French and German languages will then have the same relationship to English as Dutch and Swedish now have to them." His estimate for French was a little too low, for German a little too high, and for English much too high.

In this context, if a digression is permissible, a paradox in the attitude of the British toward the French language and literature may be noted. On the one hand, until the present century France was their traditional enemy, the country with which England was most often at war. England's finest patriotic poetry, such as some of Shakespeare and Wordsworth, was inspired by conflict with France. But French has penetrated and formed the English language more deeply than any modern European language has affected another. True, Arabic has had a similar impact on Persian and Turkish, and there may be other examples outside Europe. Yet with the possible exception of Italian in the sixteenth century, French has always been the foreign language studied by the greatest number of Englishmen, and French literature the one most familiar to them. In 1915 Robert Bridges composed his anthology *The Spirit of Man,* using both English and French selections, and it is difficult to think of any other modern European bilingual anthology.

But both British trade and the English language were helped by the spread of the empire. Unnoticed by Rivarol—or at least not mentioned in his essay—a sizable part of India had already come under British domination, and with the elimination of French influence it was only a matter of time before the whole subcontinent would find itself under British rule. With such a large base of operations, British trade and finance spread all over the Far East, and English became by far the most widely used European language in Asia. Yet what was to be the most powerful force in spreading the English language was casually mentioned by Rivarol, without the least awareness of its relevance to the subject he was studying, at the end of his essay: the British emigrants who had just formed the United States of America. David Hume had been much more perspicacious. In 1767 he had advised Edward Gibbon, who had written a history of the Swiss Confederation in fluent French, to write his projected book on Rome in English. "Why do you compose in French and carry faggots into the woods, as Horace says with regard to Romans who wrote in Greek? I grant that you have a like motive to those Romans, and adopt a language much more generally diffused than your native tongue: but have you not remarked the fate of those two ancient languages in following ages? . . . Let the French, therefore, triumph in the present diffusion of their tongue. Our solid and increasing establishments in America, where we need less dread the inundation of Barbarians, promise a superior stability and duration to the English language."

In contrast, the spread of French was greatly restricted by the low birthrate and population pressure in France, and by the reluctance of the French—compared to the British, Spaniards, Portuguese, Russians, and Chinese—to emigrate from their beautiful and fertile country. Even France's pursuit of "demographic colonization," as in Algeria and Tunisia, was unsuccessful and most of the "pieds noir" were of Spanish, Italian, and Maltese origin, though completely gallicized in culture.

The first effect of the growth of the United States was to double the number of English-speaking people to some 75 million by 1870, or about twice the number of francophones, and today the United States accounts for some two thirds of the total number of anglophones. Second, American trade with the Far East, though far smaller than British, helped to spread English in that region; the same was true, somewhat later, of American trade with, and investment in, Latin America. But the worldwide cultural impact of English did not assume significance until after the First World War, and only began to exert its full force in the 1940s, as the United States rose to economic, military, political, and scientific preeminence.

American participation in the First World War ensured that English would be used, along with French, as an official language at the Peace Conference. American industry was already the world's largest by the 1880s; in the 1920s, and once more in the 1940s and 1950s, it accounted for more than 40 percent of total world output—a figure comparable to that of Britain a century earlier. Eventually the United States became the largest trading nation, and world financial leadership passed from London to New York. Americans forged ahead in sicence and technology; American universities rose to the first rank and, by their sheer number, exerted a far greater influence than those of any other nation. American literature, music, and painting evoked worldwide attention and interest. The effect of all these achievements was multiplied by a lavish United States exchange policy—which not only helped its own citizens to study abroad but enabled foreigners to enroll or reside in its universities and scientific institutes, attracting hundreds of thousands of students.

In addition to all these aspects of high culture, the United States has had an even greater impact at the mass level. American films, TV, jazz, blue jeans, and other manifestations of "pop culture" have had an irresistible asppeal to the youth of the world (including those who are strongly anti-American in their politics), and have percolated through the tightest iron and bamboo curtains and Islamic screens. Add to all this the presence of millions of American soldiers in Europe and Asia during and since the Second World War, plus the fact that English had become the common language of the Allied troops—with an effect similar to, though incomparably greater than, that of the French Revolutionary and Napoleonic soldiers.

As a result, English has displaced French in almost all its former strongholds: Russia, Eastern Europe, the Balkans, the Middle East, and Latin America as well as Asia and the Far East. Only in North Africa and the former French and Belgian colonies is French still the second language, and even there the use of English is spreading rapidly. To continue the passage from the *Economist* quoted at the beginning of this article:

> A study published by *Le Monde* showed that of the 270 million people around the world classed as francophone, only 90 million actually speak French. Among the so-called international languages, French thus trails English (350 million), Spanish (200 million), Arabic (120 million) and Portuguese (115 million).
>
> Still, French retains great prestige. . . . A third of the delegates at the United Nations rely on it to express their views. In the light of the Rigaud report, the French foreign ministry has now taken on the task of supporting the use of French at a realistic level. It will dig in as second language in Europe, Latin America and part of the east.

It may be added that traces of the respect enjoyed by French as the language of polite society still remain. Around 1943 an American professor, along with another American, was caught too close to the Russian zone in Iran and taken to the police for questioning. His very fluent Russian did not impress the sergeant in command or persuade him to release the two. However, when the professor wished to tell his companion something that would not be understood by the Russians, he said a few words in French. "What was the language you were speaking?" asked the sergeant. "French." "Then you must be a cultivated man." "But what is so remarkable about French? I speak Russian" (and, he might have added, a dozen other languages). "No, Russian is like English, a world language, but French is a language of culture." In 1967, in Isfahan, a French-educated Iranian conceded to me that English was useful as a commerical language, but he was utterly incredulous when I told him it had produced the finest poetry in the world. And in Algiers, in 1965, I searched in vain for books in any language other than French. Even Arabic books were found in only two shops, one selling Egyptian and the other Lebanese publications. Things have, however, changed a little since then.

Three more examples of the shift may be given. In the 1970s the Soviets opened a cultural center in the Chilean town of Antofagasta, known as the "Red Port" because of its strong communist element. At that center the first thing the local inhabitants asked for was courses in English! More recently, I asked a Japanese who does a lot of business in China what language he used; his answer was "English, of course." And when Giscard d'Estaing and Helmut Schmidt used to get together and make disobliging remarks about the Anglo-Saxons, they did so in excellent English.

Needless to say, this state of affairs will not last indefinitely. Someday Chinese may assume a position more in line with China's great cultural past and its increasingly powerful present. But, at the risk of being as complacent and unperceptive as Rivarol was 200 years ago, one can safely say that for many decades to come English will maintain, and may even slightly improve, its position as the leading world language.

NINE

CHANGE IN WESTERN PERCEPTIONS
OF THE ORIENT SINCE THE
EIGHTEENTH CENTURY

Between the eighteenth and nineteenth centuries a drastic change took place in Europe's perception of the Oriental civilizations. In the eighteenth century, it had been one of respect, and often admiration. In the nineteenth, except for a few individuals, this was replaced by contempt. This statement applies to both India and China; relations with Islam were more complex and require separate and fuller treatment. The reasons for this shift were complex and include economic, political, military, technological, social, and religious factors.

Regarding India, "In the imagination of Europe, India had always been the fabulous land of untold wealth and mystical happenings with more than just a normal share of wise men."[1]

China stood even higher in European esteem, as may be judged from the very favorable references to it by Leibnitz, Voltaire, and other eighteenth century luminaries. This esteem was largely due to the writings of the Jesuits, who had worked in that country and who published the *Lettres édifiantes et curieuses*, which gave a highly sympathetic account of Confucianism and of Chinese institutions in general. The *philosophes* much preferred China's "natural morality" to Europe's religions and contrasted its toleration with the sectarian, fanatical, persecuting Christianity of their countries. China's low esteem of military prowess and high opinion of intellectuals also appealed to them. So did the fact that its government was based on merit, tested by examinations, instead of the ranks and privileges of

Europe. In 1731 a publicist, Eustace Budgell, described China as "the largest, most populous, and best governed country in the world."

Well before the middle of the nineteenth century, these attitudes had sharply changed. India was now the land of chronic famine and the source of the plagues and epidemics that afflicted Europe. It was the prime example of abject poverty conjoined with the fabulous wealth and ostentation of the Maharajahs. It was the land of grotesque idolatry, the caste system with its untouchables, of the juggernaut and of suttee. In his famous Memorandum on Education, Macaulay did not hide his contempt for Sanskrit, Persian, and other Indian literature. As for China, two quotations may suffice. Shelley, one of the most radical, most intelligent, and well-read members of his generation, was an outspoken champion of oppressed peoples. Here is his judgment on China, in his preface to "Hellas" (1821): "But for Greece . . . we might still have been savages and idolaters; or, what is worse, might have arrived at such a stagnant and miserable state of social institution as China and Japan possess." And in 1865 the great liberal Tocqueville, mocking the infatuation of the eighteenth century with China, referred to it as "ce gouvernement imbécile et barbare, qu'une poignée d'Européens maîtrise à son gré."[2] By then China was the land of immobility, devastating floods, massive famine, and opium addiction. Tennyson found few contradictors when he said, "Better fifty years of Europe than a cycle of Cathay."

Many factors contributed to this change. First, the economic; in the seventeenth and early eighteenth centuries, Europe was probably little, if at all, wealthier than China and, perhaps, even India. Indeed, the only attempt to estimate per capita incomes seems to put China slightly ahead, but such figures have to be treated with great caution.[3] However, the favorable opinion of Adam Smith, a shrewd and very well-informed observer, may be quoted. In two separate places, he says that China is a much richer country than any part of Europe.[4] As for India, contrasting its present miserable state under the East India Company with earlier prosperity, he says that the Indians and Chinese "derived their great opulence from this inland navigation"[5] and that the Muslim governors of Bengal "are said accordingly to have been extremely attentive to the making and maintaining of good roads and navigable canals, in order to increase, as much as possible, both the quantity and the value of every part of the produce of the land."[6]

In the meantime, however, Europe was forging ahead very rapidly, whereas India and China were stagnating or actually deteriorating, and attitudes were changing accordingly. This is clearly reflected in Hume's masterly essay "Of the Populousness of Ancient Nations," where, in the course of demolishing Montesquieu's statement that the "population of the earth is less than a fiftieth of what it was at the time of Julius Caesar," he demonstrated that, on the contrary, economic and social conditions had greatly improved. Agriculture was more widespread and advanced and industry, commerce, and navigation were much more extensive. Moreover, slavery had been abolished and orderly liberty had replaced despotism. The belief that they had surpassed Rome confirmed Europeans' feelings of superiority over other civilizations, ancient and modern. At about the same time, Gibbon put it succinctly: "the nations of Europe, the most distinguished portion of human kind in arts and learning as well as arms."[7]

Much of the growth in Europe's wealth had been due to improved technology. Until the early eighteenth century, China's technology matched Europe's in many fields. But the Industrial Revolution marked an unparalleled leap forward and gave Europeans a mastery over nature which put them in a separate category from all other peoples. One aspect of this technological advance was military, and Europeans soon became accustomed to defeating vastly superior numbers of Asians and Africans.

This made possible a vast extension of overseas dominions and, by the mid-nineteenth century, Britain ruled over the greater part of India and significant portions of the Middle East; France was subjugating North Africa; Russia was conquering Central Asia, and the Netherlands Indonesia; and China's impotence had been demonstrated by the Opium War of 1841.

Religion also played its part. The eighteenth century was the most skeptical in Europe's entire history. As Lytton Strachey put it in his essay on Mme. du Deffand, "The skepticism of that generation was the most uncompromising that the world has ever known; for it did not even trouble to deny, it simply ignored." In these circumstances it was not surprising that many *philosophes* preferred Confucianism or Islam, as being closer to "natural religion" and less encumbered with metaphysical baggage. But the early decades of the nineteenth century saw a revival of Catholicism in France and Protestant Evangelism in England. Typical of the age was Jane Eyre's cousin, St. John Rivers, with his burning conviction that the souls of the Indians were doomed to eternal damnation unless he went out to save them. Also typical was Florence Nightingale, who heard a clear call from God to go and do his work. The heathenism of India, China, and also Islam (*sic*) now became a major obstacle to a sympathetic understanding of those cultures.

Lastly, one subject has received very little attention but seems to have played an important part: the status of women. The Romantic movement, and more generally the nineteenth century, tended to idealize women as almost never before. In these circumstances, such practices as the Indian suttee, Chinese foot-binding, and Islamic harem were felt to be intolerable. More generally, as an American missionary working in Syria in 1845 put it: "The women, donkeys and camels bear the burden throughout the East."[8] This was another black mark, and a big one, against the Orient.

It is now necessary briefly to survey developments since the middle of the nineteenth century. The first change occurred in the Western perception of Japan—the remarkable modernization of Japan following the Meiji restoration of 1868 and Japan's victory over China and Russia resulted in the Anglo-Japanese Treaty of Alliance and in the recognition of Japan as a Great Power. In the course of this century, Japan's amazing economic advance and its military prowess raised it to the very top of the economic and political ladder. Today, Japan is not only recognized as an economic superpower, but is somehow perceived as belonging to the West and not the Orient—the greatest compliment that can be paid by Europeans and Americans.

China's recent history has been much more tortuous and painful. In the course of the nineteenth century internal breakdowns and foreign aggression resulted in a marked retrogression in many fields. Although there was improvement after the revolution of 1910, it was only after the Communist victory in 1949 that China received international recognition commensurate with its size and strength.

India's advance has been less painful, though often slower. Its image was greatly enhanced by the rise to leadership of such men as Gandhi and Nehru, and after it achieved independence (1947) and maintained a working form of democracy, it enjoyed a great deal of respect, and some influence, especially in the less developed parts of the world.

Europe's relations with Islam were far older, more complex, and more intimate than those with India and China. Both Christianity and Islam were offshoots of Judaism and, therefore, shared many common beliefs and attitudes. But they differed sharply on some fundamental issues, such as the Trinity, Incarnation, and Redemption, and the mutual hostility engendered by these and other points of difference was in some ways exacerbated by what they had in common. They were *frères ennemis*. Each looked at the other, saw its own face reflected in a distorting mirror, and recoiled in horror. At best, Christians regarded Islam as a dangerous Arian heresy and Muslims regarded Christianity as a pagan and somewhat blasphemous distortion of Islam. But it was not just a question of theology. From the moment the Arabs invaded the heartlands of Christianity in the Middle East in the seventh century, the two religions were almost continuously at war, a war that carried the Arabs to four unsuccessful sieges of Constantinople and to defeat at Poitiers. Indeed, in the eighth and ninth centuries Islam constituted the greatest single threat to both Eastern and Western Christendom. After that came a Christian offensive that resulted in the *Reconquista* of Spain and Portugal, the Byzantine advance in Syria, and the ultimately unsuccessful Crusades.[9]

Toward the end of the Middle Ages tensions began to ease. Trade flowed across the Mediterranean in increasing quantities and commercial considerations began to prevail over religious. Indeed, as the Venetians, breaking front with the Christian powers at the time of the siege of Alexandria in 1365, put it: "Siamo Veneziani poi Cristiani" (We are first of all Venetians, then Christians).

At about the same time Europeans began to see the Muslims in a new role, as teachers of Greek and Arab science. Roger Bacon urged the study of Arabic as well as Greek since "philosophy had been taken from both these peoples,"[10] and Averroism had a great impact on European thought.

A new act in the Christian-Muslim drama opened with the coming of the Turks, who captured Constantinople, subjugated the Balkans and converted many of their inhabitants, invaded Italy, and twice besieged Vienna. They inspired terror all over Europe, as may be seen from the contemporary literature and also from the prayers offered in churches for deliverance from the Turks. But at the same time, they also inspired respect for their unity, discipline, and promotion by merit as opposed to hereditary privilege. These factors caused Busbecq, the imperial ambassador, writing in 1555, to despair of Europe being able to stand against them. And as late as 1603, Knolles wrote of "[t]heir frugality and temperance in their diet and other manner of living, their careful observing of their ancient military discipline, their cheerful and almost incredible obedience to their princes and sultans, such, as in that point no nation in the world was to be worthily compared to them" [spelling modernized].

But already around 1600 Shakespeare expressed his contempt for Turkish government and the absence of the rule of law (*Henry the Fourth*, Part II, Act V, Scene II):

> Brothers, you mix your sadness with some fear;
> This is the English, not the Turkish court;
> Not Amurath an Anurath succeeds,
> But Harry Harry.

Racine's *Bajazet* (1671), based on information supplied by the former French ambassador to the Porte, is equally uncomplimentary. Gibbon, writing some 150 years later, would say: "The provinces of the East present the contrast of Roman magnificence with Turkish barbarism."[11]

A new dimension to anti-Turkish feeling was added by Europe's increasingly passionate attachment to ancient Greece and Greek culture, an attachment that showed itself in widespread Philhellenism on the outbreak of the struggle for Greek independence. Hegel, refuting geographic determinism, put the matter simply: "Where the Greeks once lived the Turks now live."

The development of European imperialism in the nineteenth century further exacerbated hostility between Christians and Muslims. Practically all Muslims found themselves under infidel rule, a situation to which they had not been accustomed, which disrupted their economic and social life, subjected them to alien values and customs, and caused resentments now manifesting themselves in Islamic revivalist and other protest movements.

For their part, the Europeans soon came to realize that Islam constituted the main obstacle to their rule and that local resistance more often than not was centered on the mosques or religious brotherhoods. From this they concluded that Islam was a religion opposed to all forms of progress.[12] A climax was reached during the two World Wars when hundreds of thousands of British and Allied troops were stationed and operated in the Middle East and other Muslim lands, coming into close contact with the local inhabitants and inevitably disrupting their society. Neither side was on its best behavior and neither was enchanted with what it saw of the other.

In addition, the Near East did not undergo the transformation that occurred in Japan, China, and India, which changed so markedly the Western perception of these countries.[13] Unlike Japan, it did not carry out a far-reaching modernization of its society. When it did achieve rapid growth, and even began to accumulate huge financial reserves, that was mainly due to a short-lived surge in the price of oil, which disrupted the world economy and produced fear, resentment, and hostility in the West.

Neither did it, like China, experience a profound and comprehensive social revolution. Its leaders were not Gandhis and Nehrus, but more often Khomeinis and Saddam Husains—though there were some exceptions. Most of the time, it has been ruled by traditional monarchies or military dictatorships. And the assaults by Muslim revivalists on the hard-won rights of women in so many countries have alienated a large segment of world opinion.

Again unlike India, it has not produced a very large body of natural scientists, computer scientists, and engineers. In spite of a huge expenditure on armaments, its military strength remains negligible, and it has had little success in dealing with its enemies—Israel and, in the cast of Pakistan, India. Hence, for both internal and external reasons, the image projected by the Near East—and more generally the world of Islam—has remained essentially unchanged and hostile.

In recent years, we have witnessed the revival of radical Islam in many countries, and the cultural and political clash with the West has intensified. And so the story of the age-long conflict continues.

Notes

An earlier version of this chapter was published in Charles Issawi, *The Arab Legacy* (Princeton, 1981), pp. 363–72.

1. Romilla Thapar, *A History of India.* vol. 1. (Harmondsworth, 1977), p. 15.

2. *L'Ancien Régime,* Book 3, Ch. 3 (Paris, 1967, p. 26).

3. Paul Bairoch, "The Main Trends in National Economic Disparities since the Industrial Revolution," in Paul Bairoch and Maurice Levy-Leboyer, *Disparities in Economic Development since the Industrial Revolution* (New York, 1981), pp. 3–17.

4. Adam Smith, *The Wealth of Nations* (ed. Edwin Cannan, New York, 1937), pp. 189, 238.

5. Ibid.

6. Ibid.

7. Edward Gibbon, *The Decline and Fall of the Roman Empire* (abridgement by D. M. Low, New York, 1967), Ch. 15, p. 143.

8. Quoted in Charles Issawi, *The Fertile Crescent* (New York, 1988), p. 31.

9. See Charles Issawi, "The Christian-Muslim Frontier in the Mediter-ranean," in *The Arab Legacy* (Princeton, 1981), pp. 11–21.

10. *Opus Maius III*, p. 1.

11. *Decline and Fall*, op. cit.

12. This sentiment is frequently expressed by Lord Cromer in *Modern Egypt* and by French writers on North Africa.

13. On this subject, see Cyril E. Black and L. Carl Brown (eds.), *Modernization in the Middle East* (Princeton, 1992).